BRAVE, STRONG, AND TRUE

THE MODERN WARRIOR'S BATTLE FOR BALANCE

Dr. Kate Hendricks Thomas

innovo
PUBLISHING

Published by
Innovo Publishing, LLC
www.innovopublishing.com
1-888-546-2111

Providing Full-Service Publishing Services for
Christian Authors, Artists & Organizations: Hardbacks, Paperbacks,
eBooks, Audiobooks, Music & Film

BRAVE, STRONG, AND TRUE:
THE MODERN WARRIOR'S BATTLE FOR BALANCE
Copyright © 2015 Dr. Kate Hendricks Thomas
All rights reserved.

Scripture taken from the Holy Bible King James Version.

Scripture quotations marked (NLT) are taken from the Holy Bible, New Living Translation, copyright © 1996, 2004, 2007 by Tyndale House Foundation. Used by permission of Tyndale House Publishers, Inc., Carol Stream, Illinois 60188. All rights reserved.

THE HOLY BIBLE, NEW INTERNATIONAL VERSION®, NIV® Copyright © 1973, 1978, 1984, 2011 by Biblica, Inc.® Used by permission. All rights reserved worldwide.

Although the *Chicago Manual of Style* was used as the primary guide in the editorial decisions for this title, exceptions were made to accommodate a style more accepted in the military community.

Library of Congress Control Number: 2014956413
ISBN 978-1-61314-309-4

Cover Design & Interior Layout: Innovo Publishing, LLC

Printed in the United States of America
U.S. Printing History

First Edition: November 2015

PRAISE FOR *BRAVE, STRONG, AND TRUE*

"Kate Hendricks Thomas has a rare gift of being able to blend poignant narratives (her own and those of other veterans close to her) with scholarly research in a way that brings both the narratives and science to life. She offers a wise, compassionate, and generous voice to the complexities of transitioning home from combat, warrior culture, neurobiology, stigma, balance, and faith."

—**Charles W. Hoge, MD, Colonel (Ret.), US Army, author of** *Once a Warrior Always a Warrior*

"Combining the latest research on military mental health with deft, authentic storytelling, Kate Hendricks Thomas invites us to think critically about how we typically discuss healing for veterans. Quite simply, faith matters. With a perspective informed by her own combat experiences, she makes a powerful case for the relationship between religion and health. She has written a call to action that is both smart and brave."

—**Harold G. Koenig, MD, Professor of Psychiatry and Behavioral Sciences; Associate Professor of Medicine; and Director of the Center for Spirituality, Theology, and Health at Duke University Medical Center**

"My experience with leadership development, my service as an Army officer, and my education in Positive Psychology enable me to conclude that this book highlights the skills and abilities of our nation's veterans. Dr. Kate Hendricks Thomas has not written another lament about the problems facing our veterans after more than a decade of war. Instead, this is a reminder that veterans are resilient—and assets to the nation who will strengthen our communities in the years ahead."

—**Mike Erwin, Founder and Chairman of Team Red, White, and Blue; CEO of Quiet Leadership Institute**

"Marines take care of one another. That spirit of service shines through in this book by Marine-turned-college professor, Dr. Kate Hendricks

Thomas. She shares her research on resilient reintegration for veterans with a bit of witty self-deprecation, humility, and honesty. *Brave, Strong, and True* makes a real contribution to the conversation about military mental health by providing the much-needed prevention perspective."

—**Major General James E. Livingston, United States Marine Corps (retired), Medal of Honor recipient**

"*Brave, Strong, and True* is a call to adventure for the modern warrior, where the real hero's journey begins when military service ends. Dr. Kate Hendricks Thomas provides inspired guidance on cultivating resilience to both warriors and the communities to which they return."

—**David L. Albright, PhD, Hill Crest Foundation Endowed Chair in Mental Health at The University of Alabama in Tuscaloosa, Alabama**

"As a pastor and leader, I am so excited and thankful for this resource that Kate Hendricks Thomas has written. To have her personal story woven together with academic research is so valuable. This book will be a tremendous help to church leaders throughout the United States as we help pastor and connect with our military veterans into our church communities"

—**Pastor Peter Haas, Substance Church, author of *Pharisectomy & Broken Escalators.***

"An excellent contribution, and a significant resource with rich case material and helpful information for veterans, their family members, military commanders, and health professionals alike. Thomas' book provides one of the first coherent and lucid descriptions of how combat veterans process the stress and trauma of combat, and the challenges they face when attempting to reintegrate from the battlefield to civilian life. As the saying goes, 'You can't swim across the river without getting wet.' Deployment to a war zone changes people; the question is how? Dr. Thomas answers this question completely. Thomas' book provides the reader with a rare perspective, combining the scientific rigor of a scholar with the detailed personal accounts from her lived experiences as a Marine Corps officer deployed to Iraq. This volume provides support, insight, and the knowledge of what to do with this understanding in order to help veterans be able to thrive and to use their stressful and traumatic experiences as a catalyst for growth, connection, and transformation."

—William J. Pickens, EdD, research psychologist, trauma consultant, educator, and consultant to law enforcement in areas related to police stress and trauma, and suicide prevention.

"I stand in awe and with strong admiration for Kate Thomas' courage and dedication, and the depth of personal expression she shares in *Brave, Strong, and True*. *Brave, Strong, and True* is a compelling read, rich in knowledge and devout in the delivery to advocate for a modern, promising approach to protecting, preserving, and promoting the esteemed lives of our honorable service members. This masterful piece provides constructive and compassionate energy to accelerate increased responsiveness to Kate Thomas' recommendations to harvest resiliency for transitioning service members."

—Dr. Melissa Butcher, Health Promotion Faculty and Program Director, College of Health Sciences, Charleston Southern University

"There is no better teacher than a real-world practitioner. Kate Thomas, a US Veteran and academic presents the reader with the concept of mental fitness as a new training standard. Her personal experiences on the battlefield and on the home front provide a unique, page-turning perspective. Her emphasis on pre-incident rather than posttraumatic is spot-on; reaction is never better than being proactive."

—Jacqueline Fish, EdD, Vice President for Academic Affairs at Charleston Southern University

"This book is solid from an academic standpoint, and it is written in a caring way to reach hurting veterans. The author's passion for helping is tremendous. Specific, effective, and realistic strategies are outlined with an abundance of encouragement. I highly recommend."

—Lori W. Turner, PhD, RD, Professor of Health Science at The University of Alabama

"I rarely can stay up reading after 9 p.m. This was not the case with Kate Hendricks Thomas' book. I was amazed that I read through her stories, research overviews, and statistics in one sitting. *Brave, Strong, and True: The Modern Warrior's Battle for Balance* is a call to health for those dealing with the troublesome symptoms plaguing American veterans. Having herself traversed the warrior's journey "there and back again," she offers honest and practical ways—including social support, self-care (e.g., yoga), and a spiritual practice—for our veterans to meet the challenges of returning home and continuing with purposeful lives."

—**Rob Schware, PhD, Executive Director of The Give Back Yoga Foundation; President of The Yoga Service Council; www.givebackyoga.org**

"Dr. Thomas turns the conversation about mental health in the military on its end, in a good way. What if we could train and arm service members to succeed in mental battles as we do in physical ones? Dr. Thomas calls for just that: mental fitness training programs that shift the paradigm from treatment to resilience."

—**Cate Florenz Michaud, Communications Director for The Bowen Group (thebowengroup.com) and US Marine Corps veteran**

"Kate Thomas is a woman that could easily intimidate others. Professional, bright, attractive, competent. So why wasn't that enough? Because Dr. Thomas cares too much about herself and other service members to let her story go untold. It takes guts to let others see below the surface and reveal the suffering and painful decisions her personal and professional training led her to. It takes a deep compassion and a fierce passion for making sure that others don't have to walk the same path. Dr. Thomas lived the real problems shared by many of our veterans. The solutions she offers are imminently sound and doable."

—**Robin Carnes, Trauma-Sensitive Yoga Teacher and Founder of Warriors at Ease; www.warriorsatease.org**

"With a unique blend of personal narratives and current research, Dr. Hendricks Thomas invites the reader to take a look at the real life struggles behind the grim statistics regarding the cost of military service. She goes on to make a compelling case for resiliency training, support, and awareness that would undoubtedly improve the lives of our military men and women. She manages to leave the reader feeling not only educated, but entertained and inspired."

—Carolyn Wolfe, LMFT, author of *Resident and Counselor Relationships in a Court Affiliated Residential Treatment Facility for Adolescents: The Role of Attachment;* www.carolynlmft.com

"Dr. Kate Hendricks Thomas' ability to be authentic and compassionate sharing her own powerful story affirms a message of hope and healing for our military communities as well as the need for training protocols that foster post-traumatic growth."

—Renee Champagne, Department of Clinical Mental Health, College of William and Mary; United States Air Force Veteran

DEDICATION

To soldiers, sailors, airmen, and Marines of every era, those I served with and those I have never met.

To my father and brother, the best Marines I know.

To Shane—a soldier, my husband, and my friend. Thank you for being crazy and wonderful enough to say forever to me and our son.

ACKNOWLEDGMENTS

I am grateful to my husband, Shane, for thinking up the title of this book, supporting me unconditionally, and still loving me even after a rocky writing day. I appreciate my parents and siblings for being willing to read the roughest of drafts and offer me thoughtful edits in that honest way only family can. I also appreciate greatly the colleagues who offered an academic review of this work, especially Dr. Karl Hamner, Mark Malmin, Sarah Plummer Taylor, Dr. Melissa Butcher, Dr. Maggie Shields, Dr. David Albright, Dr. Lori Turner, and Garrett Cathcart. I am so honored to work with all of you. I am in the debt of Bart and Darya at Innovo Publishing for this chance to put my words on paper, and for their professional direction and warm mission support.

Mostly, I am grateful for the community of servant leaders with whom I am honored to associate as we work on changing the way we as a nation talk about veterans' health. God bless all of you, and thank you for continuing to remind me what's important.

CONTENTS

FOREWORD

"Whatever we think of war, the crucial responsibility is to accompany the journey home of those who return and remind us that, as a society, we don't just leave wars behind."

—Dr. Rita Nakashima Brock, *Soul Repair*

Three numbers. Two minutes. One pitch. I was invited by the organizer to address a conference on faith and community about the need to work with veterans and their families for mutual benefit. So I prepared a talk. But when I arrived, the agenda had already run over and I was told I only had two minutes. They needed to get back on track. So I folded up my ten-minute speech and tucked it in my pocket. I sat for a minute and wondered what the heck I was going to say. Then it came to me. I needed to get their attention quickly and keep it. So, one pitch, two minutes, three numbers. *One*—one veteran commits suicide each day; *fifty*—veterans are 50 percent more likely than their civilian counterparts to commit suicide; and *six*—female veterans are six times more likely than civilian females to commit suicide. I had their attention. And one and a half more minutes. So I told them that these numbers tell a terrible truth, not about the toll sending our sons and daughters to war takes on them—although it is terrible—but of *our* failure to understand *our* moral obligation to help them come home. We must build partnerships with our warriors when they come home, to help them heal by listening and supporting. And we must recognize and embrace the lessons they have for us, inviting them to join us in our mission to improve our communities here at home. In essence, we must help them reengage in their lives, their families, and their communities at home. Maybe then we can reduce these terrible numbers. People of faith, as I argued, have a pivotal role to play in engaging our veterans in growth as well as healing. Spirituality, healing, and growth are inextricably entwined. In closing, I asked them to start listening and begin engaging with veterans and their families, and to partner and grow with veterans. Hopefully we have a few more allies in the calling to help veterans come home.

Over many years of working with diverse individuals and communities on health and social issues, I have come to understand, although slowly, that I need to listen in order to learn. Not always an easy lesson for an academic. As someone who grew up in a white, upper-middle class, academic family, I can never *understand* what it means to grow up poor in a crime-ridden neighborhood. But I can learn from those who have and work with them to strive to improve things for those still in that environment. And as someone who is not a veteran, although I can never *understand* what veterans have gone though, I can learn about those experiences from their stories. Stories, especially ones well told that share hard-won knowledge through powerful imagery, have been essential to how we as humans learn since the dawn of time. *Brave, Strong, and True* by Dr. Kate Hendricks Thomas tells one of these stories.

Over the past several years I have become part of the effort to correct our failure to understand what it means to bring our warriors home, choosing to accompany them on their journey home. Much of my own journey has been with Kate. I first met her on an elevator in the building in which we both worked. We introduced ourselves, and I learned she was a veteran of the Marine Corps and a graduate student at The University of Alabama studying veteran mental health. Never one to miss an opportunity, I immediately recruited her to be part of the team we were building at Alabama to plan and host the first *Service Member to Civilian Summit*. And Kate, never one to back away from a challenge, dove right in. The summit came to fruition in April 2015. It brought service members, veterans, and their families together with clinicians, policy makers, and researchers to give voice to and learn from their experiences. The summit was a success and hopefully will become an ongoing part of the national conversation on helping veterans and their families. Kate was a big part of that success. I am honored to call her friend, colleague, and teacher. In sharing her personal journey, her story is *Brave*. Through powerful storytelling intertwined with the lessons from the latest research, her voice is *Strong*. And in challenging all of us to rethink the way we approach veteran reintegration, to focus on growth, strength, and resilience, her message rings *True*. So I invite you to join Dr. Kate Hendricks Thomas on her journey and learn from her as I have.

Karl Hamner, PhD
The University of Alabama
Assistant Dean for Research in the School of Social Work
Director of the Office of Evaluation in the College of Education

"Coming home is harder than fighting in the war."

—Congressman Patrick Murphy

Part One

Climate, Culture, and Current Conditions

Chapter 1

SITUATION REPORT

Despite the vast news coverage of the wars in Iraq and Afghanistan since 2001, one figure has remained mysterious: the number of suicides among US servicemen and women, compared to combat casualties. Here's one statistic to contemplate: In 2012, the US military lost 295 soldiers, sailors, airmen, and Marines in combat in Afghanistan. But over this same time period, 349 took their own lives.

Right now, we are losing more veterans to suicide than to combat. I'm a pretty decisive person with limited ability to ask for help and zero trouble taking risks; there was a time I could have become one of those statistics.

Those figures are mysterious because even as we throw money and resources at clinical mental health treatment and blame rising rates on multiple deployments, the answers are elusive. The narrative of the "broken veteran" struggling with combat stress just doesn't ring quite true to those of us who served over the last decade, and the issue is more complicated than simple statistics can show.

I became a Marine to serve, and I loved being part of the Corps. As with anything I have ever loved intensely, the military changed and shaped me. To the casual observer looking in, the world seems brutal and intense. That casual observer isn't entirely wrong—the military is some of those things. Shared hardship and challenge are vital parts of the refining and rebuilding process that changes a civilian into a warrior. If you ask anyone who served, they wouldn't have it any other way. No one wants what comes easily or is handed to just anyone.

That process of obstacles, mastery experience, and shared suffering offers growth and transformation, but coming back to civilian life afterward can be incredibly hard. Standards are different. Camaraderie is different. Culture is absolutely different. I witnessed firsthand the toll that leaving the service took on many of us.

Stressful work environments, high rates of divorce and domestic violence, family separation, and repeated combat deployments all contributed, but the biggest reason for the reintegration problems many of us faced is cultural. We subscribe to unbalanced notions of what it means to be a warrior, and uphold silent suffering as virtue. Mistakes are shameful; pain is weakness. Saying that something is hard or stressful just isn't done.

I don't want to contribute to the silence that surrounds these issues anymore. Too many aspects of warrior culture are destructive lies we tell ourselves.

Who are we maintaining this veneer for?

What do we have to prove anymore?

Constant invulnerability is an illusion, and cultural mandates to be "together" in every way become dangerously prescriptive. We lose our authenticity in this way; we don't know how to reach out to each other when stresses start to overwhelm. Too many of us who are used to appearing strong would, indeed, rather consider suicide than admit to being human, fallible, or broken.

My own public story was of crisp uniforms, physical fitness metrics, and successes. I always looked good on paper. My private story involved destructive choices, broken doors and holes in the walls, hiding weapons in the house, and getting dragged across the living room floor by my hair. I was as far from God as a person could be but had no idea at the time.

As a Marine Officer, I was not supposed to make mistakes, feel depressed, or need help. But I did. Tough places and situations became tougher because I didn't know that people might be okay with an imperfect version of me. For too long I chose silence over reaching out to loved ones. I opted for deeply felt, visceral shame over openness and vulnerability.

When serving in the military we are trained to lead with confidence. Presenting a certain and effective façade requires some incredibly useful skills. We make decisions quickly and responsively, but these very same skills become incredibly destructive when we never learn how to turn them off. This description fits most service members. We tend to be a driven, almost comically dysfunctional, lot.

What if I told you that I am not perfect?

What is so useful about sharing our experiences with one another is that we offer each other the opportunity to say that kindest of phrases: "Me too." My story isn't heroic or rare, and I share it not because it is particularly special. In fact, it is only worth sharing in these pages because it is so common.

In writing this, I place trust in my fellow veterans and in a larger community of people who want to make things better for transitioning service members. From clinicians to community volunteers, there is a tribe of supportive people out there who want to help. Quite frankly, it is hard for me to leave the safely removed world of an academic researcher and talk about these issues in the deeply personal way I actually think of them. These are issues I usually discuss from a clinical distance, when in reality they impact my life and experiences, as well as the life and experiences of people I love.

That isn't very honest, and I am going to get really, really honest in these pages.

This book is my attempt to talk about the very real ways we can make reintegration easier for military veterans without hiding behind my formal education and the scientific method. I also hope that the stories I share with you in these pages help you understand the culture of military veterans better.

When we talk about suicide rates and how we can make things better, we typically talk about designing programs. Some programs are on point and some miss the mark. There are good reasons health professionals advocate for peer-led interventions grounded in Resiliency Theory. Those reasons are partially based on evaluation metrics and research, but they are also based on the embodied knowledge[1] of veterans who have made the rocky transition and come out on the other side willing to share their tales.

We are not alone.

The determined avoidance of care-seeking I lived through is disturbingly normal in the military community that I call home. For me, learning to do better involved stumbling by accident into the three key components required to build human resilience. My later academic study brought a wry smile to my face as I realized that the answer had always been there; I just hadn't known it when I needed to.

What if I had training in resilience before hitting rocky shoals?

To get to a healthier space, I had to make some hard choices, choices that involved leaving destructive patterns and people in the rearview mirror. It felt like dying to do so, but it allowed me space to breathe and to focus on becoming a new version of myself. Once I deliberately and consciously began stepping outside old patterns and belief systems to connect with and serve my community, embrace a healthy lifestyle, and seek and find an authentic relationship with God, the world stopped spinning in quite such an unforgiving fashion.

It wasn't a chaplain or a counselor who pointed me in the direction of wholeness, though I certainly tried those routes. I keenly remember sitting in my first counseling session with a well-intentioned professional, answering her with short sentences and half-truths. While I have great respect for clinical mental health practice, many of us are not interested in embracing the identity of a patient. I never was. I sneered at things that would have been really useful!

You can keep your couch.

I'm a true nerd at my core, and when the dust cleared in my personal life I became motivated to learn all I could about how we as veterans are talking about mental health. I went back to school for an interminably long period of time and threw myself into community-based programming and health promotion. When I really drilled down in my issue analyses, I didn't much like what I found. We are killing ourselves alone in apartments and no one is seeing any symptoms—we are *that* good at hiding out. It really isn't that services aren't available to veterans and military personnel when things become difficult, we just won't use them.

I reviewed a lot of research done by people smarter than me and found a common thread: existing gaps in mental health service provision are created largely by stigma against seeking care.

No matter what magic we do in the clinical realm, focusing on treatment requires a disempowerment narrative that is perceived as being incompatible with the cultural values of military veterans. We cannot overcome such norms by asking warriors to become patients and pop pills, no matter how dedicated, innovative, and gifted the clinician. While treatment is certainly part of the solution, it is not culturally acceptable for it to be the entire answer.

I know this to be true on both an academic and a personal level and believe we need to alter the dialogue about resilience. We must flip the current paradigm and turn words that currently connote weakness (like authenticity, self-care practices, and social cohesion) into training mandates and metrics of performance.

There is tremendous work to be done.

So who exactly am I talking about? Chapter 2 will explain the personality type that typically joins the all-volunteer military. Knowing what draws someone to service may help us understand the effects that such service has on a person later. In chapter 3, I explain the current state of mental health conditions in our military veterans as they relate to our most recent wars. Some of that information will surprise you. I also explain the complicated identity transition that takes place as someone leaves the active duty military or activated reserve status. None of these transitions happen unaffected by cultural norms. Chapter 4 seeks to put our conversations about military health and healing into context by painting a picture for the reader of warrior culture. We're a unique bunch, and to reach us one must know what we value.

We can't be content with understanding the military community and lamenting the many challenges veterans face as they leave the service. As a health promoter, I am never interested solely in bandaging problems. Prevention is part of a true treatment program. Chapter 5 seeks to offer a framework for discussing successful reintegration from a capacity-based perspective. This paradigm is grounded in theories of resilience, and the chapter reviews the ways we can cultivate resilient traits of our own.

Three specific components matter when we seek to become more resiliently able to navigate life's challenges: social support, self-care, and spirituality. Chapter 6 explains the importance of social support and shares some examples of how veterans can build new communities after serving. In chapter 7, I highlight the importance of self-care. Specific health practices provide a baseline of strength and mental fitness for us as humans. By making some basic lifestyle changes and learning to look at wellness in a holistic manner, we can grow stronger.

Faith builds resilience, and in chapter 8 I explain the evidence basis for this notion, as well as discuss how we can use the practice of our faith to become calmer, more connected, and mindful of our God-given purpose in the world. I am speaking very specifically in this chapter about the utility of *organized religiosity*. We often hear about more amorphous terms that label self-disciplining practices as spirituality separate from religion. These practices have real benefits, as well, but it is faith in organized and participatory form that translates most noticeably into health benefits.

The research on this is really fascinating and gave me pause when I first read it as an academic trained to separate faith from professional life. All of us have been given gifts that we are meant to use not for our own gratification but to be a light for others. Faith offers us more than a personal belief in God; it offers us reasons to get up every morning: community, purpose, and a call to servant leadership. This impacts us at every level. Spirituality affects not only resilience, but basic health and illness prevention. Science and spirituality intersect and physicians and theologians are finding important overlap spaces in their respective practices. We need to explore this to really understand what I mean when I claim that we are wired to be faithful and spiritual.

> While growing interest in the field of integrative medicine has raised awareness of the benefits of such health boosters as diet, exercise, natural alternatives to pharmaceuticals, complementary and alternative medicine, and stress management techniques like meditation and yoga, far too little attention has been paid to the spiritual roots of disease and the diagnostic and treatment tools that have been employed by healers for millennia to tend to the health of the soul.[2]

Knowing how to build resilience is interesting, but we need to see it done in individual lives and in larger communities to really understand how powerful it can be. In chapter 9, I recommend specifically how we can apply resilience-building protocols to the military veteran population to promote healing. I also advocate for going a step farther by focusing on prevention.

We can build resilience in the training environment of the active military, making mental fitness and resilience testable metrics. The potential return on investment for the services is clear, and the benefit to the next generation of volunteers would be immeasurable. I highlight here some exciting, nimble nonprofits that are modeling this work for us in the community sector. Their work is inspiring, effective, and should be emulated throughout the Department of Defense.

We trust one another.

We respond well to peer leadership.

Let's build solutions that offer real benefit to one another.

In the final chapter, I issue a challenge to my fellow veterans. We must let go of some of our imbalances to move into a healthy space. That means connecting with civilians, rather than eyeing them as untrusted outsiders, and letting go of our egos. We must seek to communicate across difference, even in spaces where acronyms and expletives have no place. Navy Seal and author Eric Greitens issued an admonition to his peers when he wrote that "one of the greatest dangers facing a veteran coming home is misdirected sympathy . . . It's kind poison. Don't drink it."[3]

We can embrace resilience cultivation and make choices that move us forward individually, as a community, and as a nation. Stress injury and depression are not permanent debilitations. Pain, hardship, and struggle can be character-building opportunities for posttraumatic growth that make us resilient leaders.

There is opportunity for exciting program development and evaluation in both the prevention and treatment spaces, and my hope with this book is to motivate us as community members, veterans, and health professionals to move forward in a manner that emphasizes strength, agency, and resilience in the military-connected population. Let's get away from that tired narrative of broken minds, bodies, and spirits.

We aren't broken, not by a long shot.

I believe this is the only way we can speak effectively within warrior subculture. I lived through the textbook symptoms of stress injury and depression and spent the next decade formally studying the issue through the lens of a researcher. Today, I feel strongly that there is a way to approach the issue of military mental health that doesn't require asking veterans to embrace a narrative of brokenness or to identify as a patient.

Mental fitness can be trained and cultivated in each of us. What if upon joining the Marines I had been offered training designed to increase self-awareness and promote resilience? If I had learned to frame self-care as intelligent preparation rather than indulgence, could handling the requisite stresses of returning from a war zone been easier? Why didn't I think it was important to make time for a relationship with God?

In the following chapters, I will ask these questions and more to outline a road map for reframing the current military mental health paradigm. Instead of discussing posttraumatic stress, we need to discuss posttraumatic growth.[4]

Posttraumatic stress and depression must be reframed as normal, recoverable conditions rather than diagnoses to ridicule. Regular training and assessment for military personnel can include a mental fitness emphasis, becoming a metric to which all are trained and tested. The research is clear: we need to alter our dialogue about mental health for veterans and focus on resilience as something that can be learned and grown before combat and transition are experienced.

This work is deeply personal to me, and not merely because of my own experiences. Like many of my peers, I had family and friends killed or wounded badly in Iraq and Afghanistan, and have lost beloved friends to suicide or self-medicating substance abuse in the last several years. I've watched the pain. I have failed to save people I cared for.

We can do better.

I believe passionately in the use of health programming that emphasizes agency and active engagement for veterans. I know how rigid and traditional the military world can be, but change has to happen. Our current deployment rates, unconventional hidden injuries, and the increased survivability of wounds that would have killed service members decades ago call for cutting-edge treatment, care, and preparation in the training environment.

We can do this—resilience can be taught. Social support cultivation, self-care modalities, and spiritual practices are the components upon which we must rely, and we must extend a hand to one another rather than overlook existing problems. As veterans, we have to contribute to the solution and cannot look only outside our own community for an answer. A bureaucracy isn't going to ride in and fix everything.

When I left the active duty, I was twenty-eight. I finished my time in the reserves at thirty-four. Both numbers rendered me old in Marine Corps years. My generation has served its watch, but I hope we still have something to offer to those who stand guard after us.

We owe it to ourselves and we owe it to one another.

***

Alone in a quiet nursery each night, I pray the same words over my infant son. I know I am lucky to be there holding him—my life almost didn't take this course. I ask God to watch over him and to help me show him each day how proud we are of who he is already. We will try to raise him to be a person who values service to country and to community, and we remind him often to be *brave, strong, and true.*

Right now my earnest words just make him giggle. One of his favorite things to do is look quizzically at me like I am crazy.

He'll understand later.

I always end this quiet moment in our favorite second-hand rocking chair by thanking God for the beautiful gift that is my present tense—I never envisioned the joy that is life with my little family. I ask Him to help us to be lights with our actions alone.

***

Veterans are resilient leaders with much to offer. This book is my attempt to use simple, limited words and stories to ask you to care about what is happening today in the community of American military veterans, and to care in a way that makes sense to us. Veterans aren't broken, and we aren't looking for thankful sentiments. We need to reconnect with the civilian community and be reminded of the wonderful, engaged, honorable things that people in our country do every day. We want to get involved with those efforts to find new purpose. We need to find new ways to serve and new identities to embrace.

Let's get out of our own way.

29

I hope my intent shines beyond the limitations of my storytelling ability, because that I am here in a quiet nursery with a sleepy child is a blessing. It almost didn't happen.

Chapter 2

MAYBE YOU CAN BE ONE
OF US

The recruiting commercial would have captured anyone's attention, especially a twelve-year-old girl who loved reading adventure novels. Glancing up from one that allowed me to "choose my own adventure," I saw a strong, handsome guy flit across the television screen. He was too old for me, but I was twelve and starting to notice boys, so I set my book on my lap and watched as he scaled a rock wall and clambered atop a mountain.

Do you remember those recruiting commercials? If you ever saw one, I guarantee that you at least thought about running off to join the Marines. The hero climbing the rock wall made it look effortless and challenging all at the same time. At the top was a fire-breathing dragon. Our hero was armed with only a sword, but a few swipes later lightning flashed and in a moment of triumph over the mythical creature he turned into a Marine wearing a sharp uniform. In that lightning flash, he became more than a slayer of dragons; he became the embodiment of honor, courage, and commitment.

I'm in.

I wanted simultaneously to hang out with him and to be like him!

If you have a heart for adventure and an appetite for challenge, you might consider the ideas of heroic dragon killing and becoming a Marine kind of exciting. A certain type of person is drawn to joining the military, despite the fact that the Marine Corps cannot provide anyone with actual dragon-slaying opportunities.

Whatever. I get the metaphor.
I'm still in.

As we consider the question of how to help veterans return to life as civilians, we must consider how they first entered a life of service. What makes someone sign on the dotted line and agree to train harder than they ever have, go anywhere, and sacrifice whatever is asked?

***

The contemporary military's missions are varied and diverse, ranging from drug interdiction and short-term humanitarian aid missions to conflicts overseas. To meet our nation's requirements, active duty and reserve branches staff, train, and equip forces in readiness that include the service branches that fall under the Department of Defense (Army, Navy, Marine Corps, and Air Force) and the Coast Guard, which falls under the Department of Homeland Security (DHS). Each service branch has a slightly different culture, but there is a lot of overlap in training requirements and missions.

***

I grew up in a family where serving in the military made sense, primarily because we grew up with a military dad. Anyone on active duty will explain that the military is more of a lifestyle than a job. As such, your work tends to come home with you and impact basically everything you do.

It is not just what you do, it is who you are.

Military culture was part of our home life from birth. As kids, we got assigned summer book reports that my father graded. We would read a book and try our hardest to write a brilliant report, pecking away on our new computer and trying not to make spelling errors. I always earned a grade of D or F on my first try, which was hard for a bookworm like me to accept. While it felt like a big, fat blow to my academic ego, my father meant it as a learning experience. He asked us to seek excellence at all times, even if we thought we were already there. He had no problem letting us cry as we chafed at the challenge presented.

We were an organized and hard-working little tribe—or else. My siblings and I still joke about the black trash bag that came out on weekend mornings when we had failed to pick up toys. We only had to see one favorite truck or doll thrown away before we learned to keep our gear in order!

In truth, our family might have been a little more intense than normal because my father was a career Marine. He was dedicated to the Marine Corps in the true believer way that a career officer must be. An Infantry Officer, I remember him coaching our soccer teams and compelling all of us to run laps while singing cadence. No one ever showed up for soccer season out of shape when he was coaching.

We had fun with the intense culture a lot of the time. I can remember one childhood Christmas morning that my family rose early, opened presents, then looked outside to see new snow falling. It was beautiful and we decided we needed to go enjoy it. The whole family bundled up and we headed out to our residential street. By then the light snow was coming down more like violent hail and sleet. My little sisters rode their bicycles, and the rest of us started off on a jog.

The neighbors told us later they thought we were crazy—a ragtag group of six running along the neighborhood streets on Christmas morning, dodging hail, laughing, and breathing hard. I remember that day as uncomplicated happiness. We were cold and wet and happy to be together making a big mess of our running shoes. The feeling was visceral and childish—it was joy.

***

In the age of the all-volunteer force, the total number of military personnel is over 2.7 million strong, including 1,453,436 active duty personnel and 1,315,445 reservists. Women comprise 14.5 percent of the active component, with fewer in the Marine Corps and more in the Air Force. The numbers in all service branches have risen every year.

For both women and men, veteran status is related to age. Historically, higher proportions of the American citizenry served at least one tour in the military. The significant majority of American men aged seventy-five and older are veterans, compared with no more than 12 percent of those younger than age thirty-five. The opposite is true for women, who are less represented in older eras of military service. Younger women are slightly more likely than older women to be veterans, but veteran status does not rise much above 3 percent in any female age group.[1]

Fewer serve today. During the last twenty years, the American veteran population (both male and female) has steadily declined. What this means for today's veterans is that only about 12 percent of their male peers and 3 percent of their female peers served during the last decade of war. Veterans return to a civilian community that has not experienced American involvement in Iraq and Afghanistan in the same personal manner. Though we are warmly received, a distant "thank you for your service" can ring a bit hollow.

***

My decision to join the Marines wasn't a tough one. The idiosyncratic messages of warrior culture made sense, and I must admit that in my military family, "civilian" was a pejorative term, synonymous with entitled laziness or apathy.

What do you mean "this is hard?" You sound like a civilian.

When we were whining about something or telling on a sibling, it was the worst thing a parent could say to us. After such childhood social conditioning, there was never a question in my mind about whether I would sign up.

In a lot of ways, I joined the Marine Corps in college to test myself. Sometimes I wondered whether I could handle the physical things I would be asked to do. I doubted whether twenty-mile hikes or sky-high obstacle courses were within the scope of things I could accomplish. Sometimes on my first try, they weren't, but I trained hard and threw myself at walls until they became easy to hop. I bruised my arms learning to chicken-wing over parallel bars. I surrounded myself with people a little stronger and faster to benefit from the push they offered me.

The sense of self I gained from jumping those hurdles was an invaluable gift. I believe that worthwhile things should scare us, and that we grow from taking on challenge. I was a typical competitive individualist, and I found a home among others who enjoyed that intense environment. We were drawn to the camaraderie we cultivated through shared hardship, and to the opportunity to push ourselves well beyond where a reasonable person would assume we should.

I was proud of every single bruise.

The unforgiving culture of the Marine Corps as a service branch made sense to me after the way I grew up. Being a female officer was another opportunity to do something many couldn't, or didn't. It was an opportunity to demonstrate temerity and to perform well against stereotype expectations.

I was young, and image was really important to me at this point, if I am being honest. I was all ego and contradictions. For example, I cared about how I looked in totally competing ways.

I was supposed to be a girl and a warrior.

I wanted to be a stereotypically pretty woman—I liked the social capital that accompanied embodying a given aesthetic. I also wanted to be an athlete who didn't waste her time with a blow dryer, to be seen as fast, fit, and completely above girly vanity. I wanted to be competent, smart, and brave on the inside, but I also wanted to be seen that way by the rest of the world. I wanted to be a good person, but I didn't want to dedicate a lot of time or study toward figuring out what made someone good.

I became a military police officer because it was as close to combat arms as a female could get, and I wanted to be a "real" Marine. I don't know where I got that definition, but I was trying to prove my toughness. To this day, I am not sure to whom I was trying to prove it.

I was a performance junkie well before I joined, but the competitive environment of the Marine Corps supported that path. I felt like I had a clear understanding of what success looked like as a Marine Officer. I had to be fast, competent, forceful, and attentive to the people I worked with. With varying degrees of success, I tried to be a servant leader and to model for others what I was asking them to do.

In those early years as a Marine, I got very good at presenting a veneer of stoic professionalism while feeling something different inside. The first time I counseled someone old enough to be my parent, encountered blatant misogyny from a supervisor, or made a decision I wasn't sure about, I quaked inside but never let it show. Presenting the certain, effective façade required some incredibly useful skills—I would only learn much later that these were skills that become incredibly destructive when you never learn how to turn them off.

I tell you all of this not because it is particularly interesting. In fact, I would say the above description fits most young people drawn to military service. We tend to be a driven lot. I only share it to give you some idea why I made the later mistakes I did. It took me years to learn anything from them, and even longer to talk to anyone about them.

These were the personality traits and supporting cultural values that allowed me to stay quiet in a dangerous situation where I needed to ask for help, and to sit mourning loss alone in a dark basement with only a case of beer and some dark thoughts to keep me company.

But always, *always*, I looked like I had it all figured out in public.

Chapter 3

MENTAL HEALTH AND MILITARY VETERANS

He called me often late at night. I always had my cell phone on and close by in case he needed me. I usually slept with it by my pillow so I would be sure not to miss him. I knew it was very possible he would wind up in trouble somewhere.

I was tired a lot.

Sometimes he would be drunk or high, wanting someone to tell him it was all going to turn out okay in the morning. One time he wanted me to go back to sleep but asked me to just leave the line open so he wouldn't be alone. I did.

I always did.

I think part of me always expected a call from some emergency room or from his family sharing news of an overdose. When I left earlier that year, he had angrily thrown at me the accusation that "I was leaving him for dead." I know that I believed him, mostly because I just couldn't bear to turn off that phone.

This time the call was different. "Will you tell a Veteran's Administration social worker that you will take possession of my guns? I need someone to vouch for my safety before they will let me go home from here." He was in Atlanta at an inpatient treatment facility.

Finally.

After years of battling some sort of mental health condition and accompanying self-medicating tendencies he had checked himself in at the VA hospital. He was tired and alone and afraid he might finally kill himself.

I packed my car and was on my way immediately, reading about protocols for visiting a patient on the lock-down ward by the afternoon. I followed the signs in the massive hospital complex to the inpatient mental health ward. A shiver went through me as I noticed the layers of locked doors and the signs warning visitors about coming in with certain items.

As the doors opened, a shrill buzzer sounded. I heard locks turning and for a long moment felt like running. This wasn't a world I was comfortable with—there were seriously mentally ill people beyond these doors!

What was I thinking in coming here?

Divorced doesn't mean I don't care anymore . . .

Sometimes I wish it did.

I swallowed hard and stepped in and through the doors, no purse or pen with me. He knew I was on my way—he could always safely assume I would show up when asked, no matter what had happened the last time we saw one another.

He needs me.

He was waiting for me past all the buzzers and locks. I saw him standing there in his brightly colored jumpsuit and tried to wrap my mind around where this had all wound up. He looked like a prisoner, and he sort of was one.

How could someone so beloved wind up here?

Was he the person I knew anymore?

Then he smiled. I recognized that wide smile, and I exhaled with relief.

***

Concern about military suicide rates and mental health seems to abound in popular media lately, but our understanding of those issues is limited and one dimensional. Specifically, the current medical model asks us to talk about veteran mental health from a clinical standpoint.

Allow me to offer my disclaimer here: Clinicians do valuable work, in particular the professionals who deploy with the military to work in combat stress units. They offer an expert shoulder and have saved lives. In no way do I disparage their noble, effective work. However, any clinical practitioner will tell you that it can be tough to get military personnel in their doors. For this reason, medical treatment can't remain the only conversation we are having about mental health in the military.

The medical model asks veterans struggling emotionally to label a problem and identify as being in need of some sort of help. We use diagnostic labels like Post-traumatic Stress Disorder (PTSD) or major depression to mark a veteran as permanently disabled; the Veterans Benefits Administration awards obscurely derived numeric ratings to men and women demonstrating symptoms. With a letter in the mail, one learns the exact percentage of "damaged" they are.

In some ways, this represents progress. Stress injury and depression are real, and pre-Vietnam they were often discussed as nothing more than cowardice or moral failure. In other ways, this readiness to label is a benevolent poison that tells veterans their normal and adaptive symptoms after military service constitute permanent debilitation. It sets up stereotype expectations of brokenness in the public consciousness and asks the veteran to rely on therapeutic and pharmaceutical interventions to get "fixed." It talks about stress as a dangerous cause of injury rather than an opportunity to hone leadership, performance, and focus under fire.

Studying mental health can be a complicated process, as symptoms manifest on multiple levels and vary greatly from one diagnosed patient to the next. Even the words we use to describe the symptoms vary greatly. Professionals discussing the same stress injury symptoms may refer to Post-traumatic Stress (PTS), the more-stigmatizing Post-traumatic Stress Disorder (PTSD), stress reaction, battle fatigue, operational stress, or shell shock. These trauma and stress disorder diagnoses are often accompanied by symptoms of depression in varying degrees of severity, and this co-occurrence may or may not be understood, recognized, or diagnosed.[1]

Depression

Depression is a diagnosis that covers a host of symptoms, which are categorized in The Diagnostic and Statistical Manual of Mental Disorders (DSM-V) by duration of symptom presence. Mild depression involves symptoms manifesting for more than four days, moderate depression for slightly longer periods, and major depression involves symptoms present almost every day for one month.

As with most psychological illnesses, symptoms manifest differently in every individual. Depression red flags include feelings of sadness, grief, worry, and tension, and possible interference with daily activities as a result of these feelings. Some people experience loss of appetite or sex drive, while others go the opposite route and overeat or engage in promiscuous or risky sexual behavior.

Highly variant, depression is often ignored or even misdiagnosed, particularly in milder forms where treatment is most effective but diagnosis hardest to pin down. Depression in some people looks a lot like stress injury, which is a normal and adaptive response to excess threats, whether those threats are present in the moment or are being reexperienced mentally in a flashback. In fact, stress and anxiety are symptoms of depression and in some patients both conditions occur at the same time. The diagnoses are different, however.[2]

Stress

Understanding stress injury requires understanding the absolutely normal way that our bodies respond to stressors. When something is at stake, we feel pressure to respond in some adaptive way. The brain tells our bodies to spring into action and sets in motion a chain of physical reactions. The human endocrine system is artfully wired to fire off a series of hormones whenever the brain registers something as threatening. Threats for a human are varied in terms of seriousness, but all trigger this exact same hormonal reaction in varying degrees of intensity.

The strongest reaction is the survival response known commonly as "fight or flight." This reaction gets the body ready for physical exertion, sending energy and resources to systems that are needed in a fight or a footrace. Heart rate increases, respiratory rate increases, and major muscles tense. Intense alertness may save a life in an immediate threat situation, but in the long term, an excessively firing fight-or-flight stress response causes problems.

When stressed to this degree, the body shuts down nonessential systems to give energy and attention to major muscle groups, heart function, and breathing. If you are running from a lion, this physical state is very useful. However, the body also considers complicated thinking, muscle repair, reproductive functions, blood flow to fingers and toes, and digestion nonessential. Over time, problems arise as the body struggles to balance competing messages.

Resources and blood flow to systems not necessary in extreme scenarios decrease. The immune, reproductive, and gastrointestinal systems are all examples. Ever get nauseous during an argument with your partner? Your body is responding to the prompting of stress hormones to stop digestion. I start forgetting things when I am under pressure for too long—I can never find my keys and might leave a cup of coffee on the roof of my car while I drive away. My brain is receiving fewer resources to do cognition during such survival-mode periods. We're not our brightest or most functional under fight-or-flight stress, which is why I like to do breathing exercises with my college students before I give them a scary exam.

Cortisol and adrenaline course through the bloodstream of someone in severe distress, from the infant who can't make eye contact with a caregiver to the soldier experiencing his first firefight. This response is meant to help us fight or flee and operates in a negative feedback loop, meaning the response will shut itself off once the threat goes away. However, if a given threat is overly traumatic or simply goes on for too great a time, the stress response keeps firing, sending the entire nervous system into dysregulation. That little case of stomach butterflies may become a legitimate digestive ailment. That simple forgetfulness may become legitimate trouble focusing. The elevated levels of cortisol and adrenaline present in the bloodstream of chronically stressed individuals directly impair the body's ability to shut down into restorative states.[3]

Our bodies release stress hormones in different amounts depending upon the severity of the stimulus. It is important to remember when we talk about stress that it isn't a simple "bad or good" binary. If the stimulus is not traumatic or severe, the body will respond in a couple of different ways to help us cope.

A particularly useful response is often referred to as the "stress challenge" response. Here, stress hormones (endorphins and adrenaline) are released at levels appropriate for promoting focus, energy, and drive to accomplish a task under pressure. I've had many students tell me that they cannot write a paper until the night before it is due. While I will never advocate for academic procrastination, they are displaying the stress challenge response as the pressure of the looming deadline prompts their system to power up.

Another common response is related to moderate release of stress hormones and an elevated level of oxytocin, the bonding hormone. This response is called the "tend and befriend" response, which involves people exhibiting extremely prosocial behavior when placed under some sort of pressure, particularly one related to a relationship. Here, we respond to our stress hormones and oxytocin by defending our loved ones or seeking help and connection from others. This response is what makes you want to call your best friend after a conflict at the office—you are seeking social support to cope with the pressure.

Biochemically, we grow from stress. The reason for this is an important hormone secreted during the stress response called DHEA. The job of this neurosteroid is to strengthen the brain after a stressful experience. This change can actually be seen in the frontal cortex when brain scans are conducted. Layers related to emotional control and reason thicken with exposure to DHEA over time. This growth and development process is highly adaptive if you think about it. We are meant to get stronger after facing pressure, to learn from growth opportunities, and to push our own limits.

Stress is a completely natural system response, and it has gotten a bad rap in medical circles. Eustress, or "good stress" drives performance and growth, and such pressures that are reasonable in duration and intensity help us become better, smarter, faster, and higher-performing. It is absolutely true that stress can become injurious over time, but mindset matters. I will discuss the healthy side of useful stress in detail in the final chapter of this book.

Stress Injuries

When a stressor is so severe that it triggers fight or flight and continues for too long without a recovery period, the body becomes injured and unbalanced. Our sympathetic nervous systems aggressively stay on, resulting in hypervigilance, insomnia, and a host of emotional regulation problems. A stress injury can make a person withdrawn, teary, or full of misplaced rage. Which symptoms manifest may depend only on what day of the week it is.

Interestingly, the vigilant and emotionally compartmentalized symptoms of stress injury double as essential survival skills in certain environments, which makes that injury useful (or even vital) in one setting and completely debilitating in another. A soldier's ability to dart eyes along a roadway in Iraq looking to swerve at any sign of debris or rock piles makes him a popular driver on convoys in-country. At home on the interstate it just terrifies his passengers.

Stress injury can certainly be a result of a one-time traumatic experience, but it can also be a result of chronically elevated hormone levels that cause the nervous system to remain in the "on" mode all the time. Anyone subjected to recurring threats of death over time is at risk of developing issues because their stress response will start staying on all the time. This abnormal stress reactivity and chronic stress response elevation becomes a stress injury, or PTSD in clinical circles.

A fight or flight impulse that never goes away can wreak havoc on the human body. Case studies conducted by Dr. Jha of the University of Pennsylvania studied long-term cognitive changes in soldiers and Marines post-deployment, looking at how stress reactions either enabled or impaired mission effectiveness. She found that in Iraq, the intensity made sense because the fast-moving landscape of the contemporary combat environment trains service members to respond quickly and to spend most of their time in elevated states of alertness. Those states persisted up to two months after coming home, however. This is where her team found the Marines struggling with focus, anxiety, and emotional outbursts.[4]

As previously mentioned, emotional reactivity is a hallmark symptom of a stress injury and can cause a vicious cycle of problems for sufferers as they create rifts in their support relationships. Dr. Jha discovered that the reason for such reactivity is that long-term stress injury decreases something called working memory capacity. This higher-level brain function emotionally regulates us, allows us to bond and interact with one another socially, and makes advanced, intellectual activities like calculus possible. Losing working memory capacity can cause a host of emotional and behavioral problems and result in major issues with attention, focus, and regulation of responses.

In addition to mental, stress injury symptoms can be physical, including among others: numbness in hands and feet, stomach problems, and high blood pressure. Though clinicians label it an injury, the body is only responding naturally to the messages cortisol and adrenaline are sending. The overactive stress response becomes ingrained in a patient with PTS symptoms, and a constant state of reactivity and hyperarousal can begin to feel normal.

How Large Is the Military Mental Health Problem?

Statistics on PTS in veteran communities are uncertain, with estimates out of the Veteran's Administration sitting at 15–50 percent. A RAND corporation study recently showed numbers hovering at about 20 percent. As one can derive from examining such wide reporting ranges, both stress injury and depression rates are largely unknown, and diagnosed depression is subject to semantic debate in the military community because symptom overlap between depressive conditions and stress injuries often leads to misdiagnosis.[5]

Here's the problem: when we talk about stress injury and depression as disorders, we give them an inaccurate air of permanence. Both occur along a spectrum of severity. At the mild and moderate levels, behavioral health treatments and professional intervention can reverse the tide. Our fearfully and wonderfully made body is meant to return to a balanced state of nervous system regulation, and mild and moderate PTS is a reversible injury. The term *disorder* is a misnomer at these points. Depression isn't a permanent condition either. This should motivate health professionals to catch conditions and intervene in advance of Post-Traumatic Stress Disorder or Major Depressive Disorder, when interventions become more about managing a chronic condition.

Are All Veterans Struggling with Depression or Stress Injury?

Contrary to some popular conceptions, stress injury is not an inevitable result of military service during wartime. In Israel, a country where every adult serves in the military for two years and war has been a common occurrence, rates of stress injury sit as low as 1 percent.

Not everyone exposed to trauma or combat suffers from reactivity issues afterward, and many mental health issues are not causally linked to trauma. Misconceptions about "damaged war vets" actually contribute to stigma issues in veterans and to feelings that only certain people, with certain service histories, "rate" emotional struggles. In fact, combat exposure doesn't predict the likelihood that a veteran will commit suicide. Among younger veterans of Iraq and Afghanistan, the greatest predictor of suicide is not deployment but rather a recent separation from service.

The reason for this lies in our human wiring. We are built to connect and commune with one another. When people cooperate and bond in close-knit groups, they increase levels of "happy hormones" like oxytocin and dopamine in their bloodstream. These hormones are in direct opposition to the stress hormones cortisol and adrenaline, and have the opposite effect on the body. This relaxation response is triggered whenever we make a close connection, and loneliness and social rejection immediately set off the body's threat receptors.[6]

As explained in chapter 2, the veteran population in America is shrinking, and society's sense of purpose and connection to our wars of the last two decades is extremely limited. This all contributes powerfully to the higher rates of stress injury and depression we are seeing in young veterans. The issue seems to be one of alienation and isolation.

Treatment programs in the clinical mental health sector have been striving mightily over the last decade to stem the tide of service suicides. The Department of Defense and Veteran's Administration have made combating depression and stress injury a top priority, specifically because they are one of several known predictors of suicide. Conservative estimates indicate that numbers of attempts and completions have increased since 1995 and are currently hovering at twenty-two veterans taking their own lives each day, along with one active duty service member per day.

We've done a great deal to try to understand the scope of the problem. One telephone survey of 1,965 service members who recently returned from Iraq highlighted the seriousness of depression prevalence; 14 percent met criteria for PTS and major depression. A larger study the following year showed 36.9 percent of the 289,000 service members surveyed had some sort of mental health diagnosis.

Careful study of suicide risk in the military population compared to the general population shows that suicide risk is almost four times higher among young veterans than their nonserving peers, a difference made more statistically significant when analysis controls for age and time in service. Internationally, numbers indicate the same. A British study of recent combat veterans found the risk of suicide to be two to three times higher for military members than the general population, with the year immediately following discharge being a particularly risky time.[7]

Beyond the numbers, researchers have asked veterans why they feel like they are struggling with mental wellness. A qualitative study published in the *American Journal of Public Health* aimed to probe more deeply the issue of post-discharge suicide risk in young veterans. Researchers conducted interviews of recently discharged troops diagnosed with depression and conducted general surveys of separating service members who did not have a diagnosis. Their study demonstrated that major issues for veterans were reintegration into new roles and the loss of community felt when leaving the military.

Veterans described a sense of burdensomeness and extreme disconnect from civilians. These feelings linked to a failed sense of belonging and desire for death. Later studies focused specifically on female veterans and found that descriptions of symptoms and feelings of disconnect were markedly similar, though more pronounced and likely to be of greater severity.[8]

Can We Predict Mental Health Issues in Veterans?

Research efforts to find biomarkers that make someone susceptible to stress injury or depression are underway, but those results will be too far down the road to matter for my generation of veterans. In an effort to deepen my own understanding of mental health conditions in the military veteran population and to look for variables that render someone more likely to have the condition, in 2014 I worked with a team to complete a study looking for predictors of depression in a large sample of military veterans.

We wanted to examine how many of these veterans already had diagnoses of depression of any severity and discover how many exhibited symptoms that indicated they were suffering from depression that had simply not yet been diagnosed. Our results for depression diagnoses showed that 14.9 percent of veterans had been told by a medical professional that they needed help for poor mental health. Another 7.7 percent exhibited symptoms that indicated the likelihood of undiagnosed depression.

Our team at the University of Alabama split the respondents by age into conflict era, examining rates of diagnosed and undiagnosed depression in veterans from Iraq and Afghanistan, Gulf War I, Vietnam, and Korea. There were noteworthy differences in veterans of different eras. Far and away, the most likely group to be dealing with an undiagnosed condition was that comprised of recent veterans of Iraq and Afghanistan. The least likely to be depressed at all were older veterans of the Korean War generation.

We also explored demographic variables like sex, race, ethnicity, and romantic partnership status, along with behaviors like whether or not a veteran smoked cigarettes, engaged in binge drinking, exercised, or battled chronic pain. Several variables were associated with being depressed: Women had higher rates, as did veterans who smoked or drank heavily. Veterans who battled pain or who reported being completely physically inactive also struggled.

I was really interested in the concept of connection gaps as predictors of depression. Although having a romantic partner is an imperfect method for determining the level of social support a veteran enjoys, living with a partner made a respondent in this survey less likely to have a depression diagnosis or to be suffering silently with undiagnosed symptoms. We didn't know how happy that relationship was, but having someone at home offered protective benefits, regardless.

Curious about the often-discussed stigma issues, we looked at their beliefs about mental health treatment services. The results were shocking. Only 2 percent of over 54,000 respondents thought clinical mental health treatment was a helpful service that could help a person live a normal, happy life. Interestingly, stigma could be overcome with exposure and experience, and our results showed promise for the current clinical treatment services available to veterans. For example, if a veteran had a diagnosis and had been working with a mental health provider, they were twenty-four times more likely to have a positive opinion about what mental health treatment could do for a person than a veteran who had not.[9] Once they were in the door, opinions changed. The problem remains getting through the initial door.

If we know who is struggling, we can create specific programs led by stakeholder members of a specific subset of the veteran population. This research is useful in providing road maps for providers hoping to target veterans by identifying variables, and in expanding our scope of understanding concerning how to reach military veterans in culturally competent ways. Post-incident treatment must be part of the package as we work to make things better for veterans leaving the service, and we can always work on doing that better and expanding our reach and understanding.

Here's the catch with such research and practice: the clinical recovery paradigm is limited. Veterans are not excited about embracing patient identities and accepting diagnoses. The challenge for health professionals looking to stem the tide of service suicides and improve quality of life for veterans lies in shifting from a focus on problems toward a focus on capacity building. In this space, we may have massive opportunity to make a positive impact. Focusing beyond labels and therapy and relying on theories and methods of resiliency, cultivation, and preparation are key.

To do those things well, one must understand the culture of warriors.

Chapter 4

WARRIOR CULTURE

In truth, it is wildly antithetical to military culture to admit to needing help with anything, particularly a nuanced, misunderstood problem like mental health. Depressed veterans face inexorable stigma when it comes to care-seeking for a possible or confirmed condition. This stigma shapes behaviors and choices, and the pressures come from within as much as from the surrounding environment.[1]

We joke in the Marine Corps about "drinking the Kool Aid," which simply means thoroughly embracing the culture and lifestyle. Everything is intense, and we are demanding of ourselves and one another. When you're serving, you are a part of an insular tribe. The commitment to a shared set of values becomes comfortable and feels automatic—unquestionable even. Many of these shared and reinforced values involve strength and dependability, and it becomes comfortable to work to be those things at all times.

I did well within that system for a long time, never realizing that my attachment to a self-image of dependability was so strong that it was tilting me dangerously off balance. It isn't something you realize until that self-image becomes threatened.

My story started the way many do, with sparkly attraction that morphed into friendship, then into love. It was the sort of love that changed the way one saw the world. Unfortunately, my story also ended the way too many do, with holes in the walls, broken doors, and police knocking at the front door.

I met Kyle by accident—I hadn't even planned to go out to dinner with my friends that evening. I walked up to the table with hair casually tossed into a ponytail and zero expectations. He smiled at me, and he had a smile that seemed to light up the room. I remember that being my first impression—a wide smile and lots of very white teeth.

I still grin when thinking about that first dinner and the way our eyes meeting felt like an electric shock to my entire body. There was a knowing in our eye contact, and it seemed like the decision to become inseparable was made for us both in that instant. Kyle made me laugh at every turn. He was charming and outgoing—the life of every party. It seemed to me that his dynamic personality lit up every room he walked into.

We were both Marine Officers, which meant he understood my work world. I can't tell you how ridiculous it was to try to date a civilian guy as a Marine; I got so many crazy comments, odd looks, or would-be boyfriends who couldn't understand why I was *still* at the office. My job demanded long hours at least six days per week. I often slept in the field or had overnight duty, and it was a relief to spend time with a man who understood a schedule like that.

We worked hard and played even harder, which was all perfectly normal in the Marine Corps. Free time was a rare commodity, making us feel like every night out should be as epic as possible. We were sensation seekers who were always up for a challenge or adventure. To us, epic nights out often meant heavy drinking and keeping late hours at bars.

Kyle and I got serious quickly. Lots of us on active duty did that. Someone was always deploying and those outside circumstances often forced big questions and placed premature pressures on military relationships. Soon after we started dating, Kyle was packing bags to head overseas again, and we had to make quick decisions about what we were to one another. Moving in together, getting married, and spending as much time together as the Marine Corps allowed wove the tapestry of our early relationship, and we were at once both wild and wildly happy.

It is hard to explain what my tie to Kyle felt like. He was the first person I shared almost everything with, and he was never judgmental. The guardedness that characterized my professional life of course seeped into my personal life, and I had always shown boyfriends incomplete versions of myself. For someone unaccustomed to sharing, doing so felt cathartic and bred feelings of closeness that allowed me to ignore certain things.

First came the red flags that I ignored because I had all the same problems. Kyle drank in binge fashion, early and often. He was reckless and took risks at any opportunity, always up for some untried, new experience. Most of the time, I was right there with him. If you only had one day off or were counting down the days until your next overseas rotation, it didn't seem unreasonable to drink all day long or find something crazy to do in order to maximize your limited play time.

Then there were the flags that I somehow chose to ignore and excuse because I was blindly smitten. Kyle would mix prescription pain medication with alcohol, or go out late and head to work without sleeping at all. One night he was gone until 4:00 a.m. and couldn't explain where he had been. He had dark periods of time where he would disappear into himself, crawling into bed for days and taking NyQuil to stay asleep.

It still seems embarrassing to admit out loud that I didn't see the downhill slide. I was at once too busy and too proud. At the time, I didn't see Kyle's behaviors as symptomatic of anything larger than boredom or a bad attitude, and I railed against each one with righteous anger. It became a cycle of fights, promises, and forgiveness that was always on repeat.

I also stayed very good at keeping up appearances. When one of his angry outbursts left a foot-sized hole in our wall, I moved furniture and arranged pictures to cover the damage. When family and friends came to visit, I had clever explanations for why the doors in our house were off the hinges. Loud yelling became shoves into walls or furniture. Drinking became hard drugs like cocaine or benzodiazepines.

Our fashionable apartment and put-together life started coming apart, and my self-denial got harder to keep up. One sunny afternoon, he dragged me across the living room floor by my hair and threw me out the front door. I remember being glad that our industrial-style concrete floors were smooth and polished—at least I slid easily.

I can't even recall why he was angry. The neighbors who called the police never asked me any questions, and I never offered them anything but averted eyes. I couldn't tell anyone about it, even as forgiving and forgetting each incident was getting harder and harder to do. I was all alone at this point by choice. I was too invested in seeming smart at all times, and I knew smart women weren't supposed to have problems like these in their relationships.

The influence of culture on my behavior during that period of time and on behavior in general cannot be understated. It never entered my mind that Kyle had a problem with depression or stress injury, and that all of his self-medication had a source. It never entered my mind to go ask someone for help with an abusive relationship that kept escalating.

Never.

I'm a freaking Amazon. These things don't happen in my world.

One's surrounding social norms play a vital role in shaping the attitudes and beliefs commonly used to delineate and define culture, and my culture was one of independence and infallibility. Only the weak had problems, and my husband and I couldn't be weak.

In insular and intense communities, normative values can become highly prescriptive and are enforced in a myriad of intangible ways. It can become tough to describe why a belief is held when cultural norms reinforce it; the belief is likely to feel like inarguable fact. Once deeply internalized, social norms become part of our ego identity and our notion of whom we are at our deepest level.[2]

Emotional norms become more than internal disciplinary tools as they are reinforced by colleagues. Such reinforcement is rendered more effective in communities with high levels of adherence to hierarchy. Especially in military communities that promote competitive individualism, this allows the expectations of others to weigh heavily on warriors' shoulders. We become committed both to serving one another and to looking "together" in our own eyes and in the eyes of our fellow service members.

As things got worse in our home, I was truly not equipped to be a real source of help to Kyle. I was as invested in presenting an image of strong silence as he was, trained and driven to disregard symptoms that were staring me right in the face. Warrior subculture tends to promote the belief that acknowledging emotional pain is synonymous with weakness and, specifically, that asking for help for emotional distress or problems is unacceptable.

Mark Malmin's anthropological work with military and law enforcement communities paints a picture that resonates with me. Years after leaving the military and Kyle, I would read his words in a journal article and gasp at their accuracy. He made plain the consequences of my cultural buy-in and explained how warrior culture can distort critical thinking and good judgment in cases where warriors suppress emotional pain, fail to apply sound cognitive thinking, acknowledge real health or wellness issues, and intentionally choose not to seek help that might remedy a mental health problem. If strength is a virtue, becoming a patient is antithetical to being virtuous.

There is nothing untoward to see here.

I've got this.

The result of such a firmly entrenched value system is feeling a whole lot of shame associated with emotional struggle, patient identity, and mental health conditions. They are simply not options. This doesn't just mean that service members deny needing help; it means that we avoid recognizing symptoms as such in ourselves or in those we are close to. If forced to address displayed symptoms, we will take denial to new heights and even actively dodge treatment when prescribed.[3]

The Department of Defense and the Veterans Administration work tirelessly to provide treatment options for service members with depression and stress injuries. Within the military community, the issue isn't lack of screening for depressive disorders, nor in the medical care available to service members suffering from depression. Rather, the problem is getting veterans to use treatment services. I was a leader who had directed Marines working for me to Family Services or Combat Stress many times.

Use them myself? Not an option.

One large, post-deployment study of reserve and National Guard soldiers coming home from Iraq revealed dismal mental health numbers. Forty-two percent of soldiers surveyed were flagged as being in need of evaluations and possibly treatment. Only half of that flagged percentage actually went to their evaluations. Of the half who did agree to seek help from therapists, only 30 percent followed the basic program through the full eight sessions.[4]

A major reason service members avoid treatment is that recommendations to seek it often come from civilian mental health providers. Because warrior cultures have their own temperaments, members are typically exclusive and mistrustful of outsiders with different life experiences. The military is an insular world, and well-

53

intentioned providers are simply not a part of it. As discussed in the previous chapter, research has shown that after deployments, separating service members feel incredibly disconnected from civilians.[5]

At no time in my military career was this feeling stronger than right after coming home from Iraq. I served with the Second Military Police Battalion in Fallujah for much of 2005. I felt most days like I was part of something important, surrounded by people I would do anything for, and that my work mattered.

The Marines I worked with meant more to me than anything in the world, and that feeling was mutual. It was proven to me in very practical ways in Iraq.

As Military Police, one of the things we spent time doing was traveling around the country to meet with Iraqi corrections officials to discuss how things were being done in their prisons. On a trip down to Al Hillah, we stayed aboard a joint base with soldiers from Mongolia and Poland. As a woman in Iraq, you are stared at frequently no matter where you are, but among the Mongolians I looked like a blonde giant and received a lot of funnier-than-normal looks and even a few requests for photos as though I were a novel alien. Some of the other looks shot my way from the Polish soldiers were less friendly, but I paid them little mind.

The day after arriving, we left the confines of the Forward Operating Base, venturing into the city of Al Hillah to visit the local prison, which happened to be one of the few facilities that held incarcerated women. The women's prison, if one could even call it that, was a single room with a drain in the center of the floor. Women of different ages were being held, some with their toddlers sleeping next to them on the concrete floor. The translator told me that there was nowhere else for the babies to stay, and no one else to care for them. Social services weren't coming to help those little ones.

Some women were there after a rape or accusation of adultery in order to protect them from family reprisal. It was heartbreaking and strange when a little girl ran up to me to be held. She gazed at me as though I were the most interesting thing she had ever seen and chattered in a language I couldn't understand. She kept running back to her mother to ask questions and point at me. I was twenty-five and not terribly maternal yet, but her sweet smiles tugged at something in me.

My job was to make some recommendations for how conditions might be improved for those women and those sleeping babies. I felt woefully out of my depth, and knew I would depart leaving little changed. One infant in particular was sprawled out, sleeping peacefully with his face pressed against the hard ground. He was sleeping the way one does when truly spent, oblivious to surroundings. His arm reached out just so to brush legs of his mother. As our gaze met, I was struck by her sad eyes. I left there feeling incredibly pensive. Was I making anything better here? Back on the base, I went to sleep holed up in a disintegrating barracks room with a plywood door. My fellow Marines were next door, and we knew we only had a few hours to close our eyes before leaving to head back to Fallujah.

Sometime in the dark of night, I clicked awake. I don't know why, but I felt the overwhelming need to be alert. I reached for my service weapon, which was reassuringly nearby, as always. Suddenly, the plywood door was shaking as someone started to pound on it and try to push it open.

The language outside the door was foreign, and their words were slurred with alcohol. The rape risks facing women on overseas bases were no secret, and I knew what was happening immediately. I assumed being aggressive would lend me a better advantage than sitting quietly while they broke the crappy door down. I moved toward it with my 9mm in hand. As I opened it to see two Polish soldiers drunkenly trying to push their way in, the Marines in the hut next door flooded out. I don't even remember everything they said, but the tone was beyond clear.

What the %^*$ are you doing here at her door?

The soldiers mumbled apologies and left hurriedly in a fit of self-preservation, both disappointed and embarrassed. I cannot remember ever seeing drunk people move that fast! I didn't feel afraid, though I knew their intentions were to try to sexually assault me that night. I was armed and I didn't need to be worried for a second with my people nearby.

I was lucky and blessed to be a part of that team.
I wish all my sisters could say the same.

***

My experiences in Iraq on convoys and with incoming indirect fire were characterized by excellent timing and good fortune; I came home totally unscathed by either contact or injury. The most I ever saw on the road was a controlled Improvised Explosive Device (IED) detonation. That is a pretty rare thing to be able to say and for many people I loved, this wasn't the case.

My younger brother and I have always been close. He was a Marine Corps Infantry Officer, and when I was near the end of my stint overseas, his was just beginning. Stars aligned when his unit flew in and I had just convoyed down to the Forward Operating Base where they were to arrive. We overnighted there, and I made sure to check the incoming flight list.

I was able to get to the hanger around the time his unit was landing and be there waiting for him. I probably had some big-sister notion about welcoming him and telling him everything he might need to know to stay safe. I still remember watching him getting off the C-130 with all his gear. He looked ten years old to me, buried in a rucksack with big, blue eyes peering out from under his Kevlar helmet. I wondered for a moment how his unit had let a kid on the flight.

My heart sunk when I saw him, and for the first time since arriving in Iraq I allowed myself to feel reality. I knew where his guys were headed and it terrified me. Ramadi was a bad place in 2005; we all knew that.

A month later, I was landing safely in North Carolina as an IED changed the world of several Marines and a young Navy corpsman forever. My brother was in that vehicle.

Thank God, he lived through the experience, though it crushed him that not everyone did. He was medically evacuated to Ramadi Surgical, then Baghdad, then Germany, then Maryland. I remember being ticked off that I hadn't known he was hurt so that I could have tried to finagle my way to him. I was peacefully packing gear not far away. The thought that he might have woken up scared or alone when I could have been there killed me. Once we were both home, I was so grateful for the chance to spend hours by his recovery bedside in Bethesda Naval Hospital—it was better than the alternative funeral at Arlington Cemetery.

For me personally, it was the beginning of a really confusing time in my life. Since I had just returned from my deployment, I had some time off that I elected to spend near him. I spent some nights in the hospital lounge, a couple with my parents at the Fisher House, and many others with family and friends in the DC metro area. I would leave the hospital some days and spend time in the "real world," but it was a world I no longer recognized. Everyone seemed so casual and happy, oblivious to the pain and sorrow facing the young men I had just left on Ward 5. I didn't know how to speak to civilians, and my resentment of their complacency seethed under the surface. I was simply angry with no articulable words for why.

I got a bit self-destructive that month. I broke up with the supportive, stable boyfriend I'd had for years because he had left the active duty Marine Corps and somehow now fell into the category of "people with different priorities who didn't understand." I spent my time with fellow Marines, partied too much, and tried not to say out loud what I was thinking about most everyone who wasn't in the service.

My struggle connecting with even well-loved friends and family whose lives were untouched by the wars was far from unique. It felt unbelievably awkward, and for me created frequent feelings of disbelief and rage. I stopped wanting to speak to anyone who didn't speak my chosen language of alienation and latent anger.

I can look back and bemoan my lack of awareness about reintegration, but having tons of skills may not have mattered either. Lots of people had the same issue. I was struck reading the story of a professional who was formally trained in combat stress and skillful reintegration. She knew more than anyone how to avoid feelings of disconnect, yet she herself was not immune. A mother and Navy mental health provider, Dr. Heidi Squier Kraft returned from serving with the Marines of Al Anbar around the same time as my brother and me to return to stateside practice. Of the experience she wrote:

> And so I returned to life as a clinical psychologist in a peacetime hospital. Despite my clinical knowledge that each individual's suffering is real and important, I often found myself staring in disbelief at my patients. I could not fathom the crises that my patients made out of their life events, nor could I empathize with the petty relationship, work, or financial stressors that brought them to tears in my office. Only months before, I had

57

held the hand of a twenty-two-year-old hero who gave his life to save two of his men. I had witnessed courage in the face of injury and pain, loyalty in the face of grief. Everyday psychological problems not only paled in comparison, they struck me as frankly absurd. Despite the personal toll seven months of war had taken, I found myself wishing I worked on a Marine base. At least then I would know what to say to my patients.[6]

The feeling that American civilian culture was just as foreign as any far-flung land stuck with me, and it prompted me to stay in the Marines when my contract was up, select a new duty station, and to move more completely into the mind-set that characterized my time with Kyle.

Both card-carrying warrior culture members who adhered rigidly to all its norms and values, Kyle and I became a dysfunctional duo in the last year we were together. We both ignored symptoms and put Band-Aids on wounds that were both figurative and literal.

Kyle's personality was unpredictable. He would go from being really energetic to very withdrawn or even angry and violent without warning. One long weekend, he cancelled our plans to see friends. He went to bed for four days and wouldn't speak or even get up to eat. I stayed nearby, confused and worried, hoping to cajole him into a happier mood.

I didn't call anyone.

The military can be hard on families and relationships in a myriad of ways, especially with a few combat deployments thrown in. Not everyone who struggles in the transition from service member to civilian has a combat history, though, which surprises many. Kyle held fairly rear-echelon jobs in the Marine Corps. I had always thought of depression and stress injuries as combat related. I knew Kyle hadn't had experiences like my brother or others had, so I assumed he was (and should be) fine. Years later, I would read that combat exposure is not a reliable predictor of mental health problems, and what impacts one person may not affect another at all.[7]

I don't think I will ever have a "why." I know Kyle felt tremendously guilty for being gone during some tough times for his family. When his father lost a long and painful battle with cancer, he was halfway across the world unable to lend anyone he loved a hand. He might have always had some issues simmering under the surface. I was simply too close to figure it out.

I'm not a psychiatrist, but to this day I cannot believe that I didn't recognize his dark symptoms. I knew he had the mood swings and sleeplessness that often come along with a depression diagnosis, but I never pushed counseling—that was something those "other, weak people" needed. I never associated him with mental illness nor considered it a possibility. I never asked myself if my own angry mental state or feelings of alienation were healthy.

Our days were very, very dark toward the end. They are a haze of alcohol and bad choices, walking on eggshells, crying, and making shameful compromises.

This isn't me.

This can't be who I am.

Is this the future I choose?

I did a lot of shameful things to try to hold my marriage together and to keep up a veneer of happy functionality. I wish I could say I was a good influence on Kyle, but I had an unhealthy approach to drinking and used alcohol as an escape from reality in all the same ways he did. I had no idea that Kyle had real problems, and that to him partying was more about self-medication than shaking off a hard week at work.

My best friend was disappearing into a sad place right in front of my eyes, and I didn't know how to see that reality, much less help him. Alcoholic, addict, depressed, unstable—these were all labels I couldn't bring myself to apply to him. I was both ill-equipped and too close to help. No matter how much I read about codependent behavior or how often I hear differently, it still feels like a failure I will always carry.

I was afraid in my own home, but I would never have labeled myself a victim of anything. I had no idea yet that I needed help, and wouldn't have known how to accept it if someone had offered.

It wasn't until one of Kyle's particularly scary benders left me alone in our apartment, searching for places to hide our ammunition that I realized something had to change. He was mixing alcohol with Valium at the time, and I could barely understand his speech. He had become paranoid, obsessively checking my whereabouts, phone records, and e-mail inbox.

I had no idea where he had gone that night, but I knew he always came back drunk. I searched for places to secret away rounds so that even if he went for one of our weapons when he came home, he wouldn't have anything to fire them with. I knew he needed help, and a tiny doubt began to creep into my mind about whether I was ever going to be able to get him to seek it before something bad happened to me. It was the first time I considered leaving, knowing I might be leaving him drowning.

Service members are conditioned to avoid recognizing symptoms that could indicate depression or posttraumatic stress. This makes perfect sense when considering the unique and treatment-recalcitrant military culture in which this phenomenon occurs. Mental health conditions are viewed as moral failures, and civilian treatment providers as benevolent but untrusted outsiders. We don't want to see depression or posttraumatic stress symptoms in ourselves, in those we love, and we certainly don't wish to seek professional help.

The results of our belief system show up in our suicide statistics. Before the wars in Iraq and Afghanistan, the incidence of suicide in active duty United States service members was consistently 25 percent lower than in the civilian population. Currently, military and veteran suicide rates exceed those found in the general population.

Providers work tirelessly to dream up new ways to treat depression and stress injury, but they can only ever provide a partial solution. The answer can't come solely in treatment form.

Too many of us won't recognize the need for professional help, seek it out, or stick with treatment if forced to go. It becomes easier to wall ourselves off from the world than to share vulnerabilities or shameful imperfections.

Without ever making any of these admissions, I filed divorce papers and packed the car. I called his sister and left her a message that asked her to look out for him without giving away any in-depth information. I was still being loyal, in my own mind.

I left everything material I owned at our former home with him and drove off, a completely broken version of myself.

Part Two

Tactical Resilience Training

Chapter 5

FROM TREATMENT TO RESILIENCE: SHIFTING THE PARADIGM

"Resilience is the natural, human capacity to navigate life well. It is something every human being has—wisdom, common sense . . . The key is learning how to utilize innate resilience." [1]

Sarah was at the tail end of her training program when it happened. She was a month away from being commissioned as an Officer of Marines. She had lived an atypical college life to pursue that goal, training hard at five in the morning instead of sleeping until noon after a night out with sorority sisters. She studied hard, broke in boots on early morning hikes, and slept in the mud during training exercises with her fellow midshipmen.

They were a small band, bound together by their desire to push themselves and earn their places in the Marine Corps. They were all close, and had seen one another through breakups, failed exams, and doubts about their readiness to complete Officer Candidates School. They were Sarah's closest friends, people she simultaneously admired and enjoyed.

She never thought it would be one of them.

She will laugh wryly and without humor today as she shares what she used to think about sexual assault. In her naïve early conception, rape was always a clear-cut act of violence perpetrated by a stranger in some dark alley. If a smart woman took steps to avoid dark alleys, she would be fine. It couldn't ever happen at the hands of a trusted friend and a member of her Marine Corps family.

But it did.

Her world could have crumbled that night, but she compartmentalized like a good Marine and pressed forward, ignoring the nagging voice telling her that she was missing something. She reported the assault and tried not to notice the way her command grilled her about the same details over and over and declined to press charges against her attacker. She spoke to a counselor, as her command recommended, avoiding medication and working hard to show her professionalism. She tried not to mourn too noticeably when those few sessions were later used to disqualify her from flight school. She tried not to notice the friends who took sides, and she simply moved forward, doing the jobs she was asked to, deploying to Iraq twice and working hard to avoid that nagging voice. The years rolled by, as they do when we don't pay close attention.

It wasn't until she was alone with her thoughts that it got really bad, and Sarah realized she was looking at her service weapon with a wistfulness that scared her. She had a choice to make: give up or do the hard work of processing a rape that felt like a betrayal at every level.

It was tempting to let the depression take hold, but Sarah had never been a quitter. She didn't really know what was next, but she knew she felt better when she moved and paid attention to her breath. So she did lots of that. She carved space for exercise and for sitting quietly afterward, letting her thoughts come as they wanted, no matter how scary they were.

That was her beginning.[2]

***

Whether a veteran leaves the active component with nothing but the happiest of memories or with a trauma history doesn't change the fact that reintegrating into the civilian world is challenging. The experience sinks some of us, and some of us it molds into new and productive people who embrace notions of servant leadership.

The question of *what makes the difference* fascinates me, both personally and professionally, probably because I was such a cautionary tale for so long after leaving the Marine Corps.

Seriously, I should have been on a salacious, daytime talk show with all my drama.

Driving away from my home in New Orleans didn't divorce me from my codependence, and I continued to spend my time and energy trying to "save" my ex-husband. I mourned our split all alone, trying to hide tears and avoid explaining anything to anyone.

I sunk into a very unhealthy state where I usually had a bottle of wine or a six-pack of beer as my only company. If you had asked anyone close to me for details of what happened, they would've had none to offer. I had shut everyone out and no one was truly close to me anymore.

Luckily, I needed to work, and my fitness background brought me to a boutique studio that would pay me well to teach size-six women how to become size fours. It got me moving and put me around people interested in wellness.

I was still aggressive in my approach to physical movement, and I pushed myself to a breaking point one afternoon in the weight room. Exercise seemed a great escape from the nagging voices of unprocessed problems, and I was there for the second time that day. As I lifted something too heavy, too quickly, and with improper form, I heard a pop and felt a blinding pain shoot through my back. I had slipped a disc between spinal vertebrae, and my body accomplished through force what nothing else yet had. That injury forced me to be still and analyze a few things. I slowed down and started to pay attention to whether my choices were in line with my values.

Did I care about anything other than myself and my broken marriage anymore?

Why was I throwing all of my effort at an addict who couldn't seem to make changes?

I used to be very involved in civic volunteer work, and in college I was always walking dogs at a shelter or planning a Take Back the Night march. I couldn't remember the last time I had done any real volunteer work, but I started to think about shifting my focus outward a bit more.

It changed everything.

And that was my beginning.

Resilience—The Theory

Any good program designed to help veterans leaving the active component needs a theoretical underpinning. Paying attention to both what has worked historically and to cultural competency saves well-meaning professionals from misdirecting resources in attempts to reach military veterans who simply miss the mark. Behavioral change theories apply what we know about human psychology, sociology, physiology, and culture to health programming.

One commonality that behavioral health models share is a focus on the audience as unique, each priority population requiring targeted interventions. The personality of the veteran population is not the same as others, and a program must be modified according to the perceptions and realities of those it is designed to impact. When working to reach veterans, one must be ever mindful of culture and that commonly understood warrior ethos that renders a focus on assets and strength more useful than one focused on susceptibility or recovery.[3]

Resilience has been most frequently defined as positive adaptation despite adversity, and few theories are more appropriate for working with veterans struggling with reintegration than Resiliency Theory. Resilience can be trained and taught and is useful for both military trauma survivors and for an average person with absolutely zero trauma history. Frankly, we can all use more of it.

The dialogue surrounding resilience is uniquely appealing to veterans. Studying resilience involves identifying the protective personality traits and behaviors that promote growth, and looking for practical ways that programming can strengthen and encourage accessing such traits.[4]

Original research on Resiliency Theory came out of the fields of social work and social psychology, but unlike more problem-oriented theories, it came about after inquiry into characteristics demonstrated by survivors of trauma. Researchers began first by asking the question of why some survivors fared better after difficulty than others who experienced the same events.

Dr. Emmy Werner spent three decades studying children labeled "at risk." In reality, the stories and backgrounds of these children would break anyone's heart. They came to Werner's social workers from abject poverty and abusive homes. Some had parents suffering with mental illness and were basically orphans. Some actually were orphans without relatives or resources to take them in. She studied over seven hundred children to look for common traits in the ones who managed to rise above their "at-risk" status. To Dr. Werner, rising above simply meant becoming an independent and functional adult, avoiding law enforcement involvement, and being institutionalized for mental health problems, substance abuse, etc.

Her research found that 36 percent of those children were thriving and achieving success in school, professions, and relationships. They self-reported high levels of happiness and quality of life. They all had some similar qualities and personality indicators, and Dr. Werner codified these as resilient traits. Kids who tested as socially responsible, adaptable, tolerant, and achievement-oriented seemed to thrive, especially if they also had excellent communication skills and high self-esteem.[5]

Follow-up studies demonstrated important resilient traits in other countries and populations, with marked similarities existing in thriving survivors. Dr. Michael Rutter's work with at-risk children in Britain highlighted the importance of having a relaxed attitude, demonstrating high self-efficacy, and having good social support in cultivating resilience. Self-efficacy is the belief that you can accomplish something, and it predicts performance as well as the ability to connect with others.

Efficacious people are more likely to engage in preventive behaviors, adhere to desired changes, and view new challenges as eustress rather than distress. Efficacy is built several ways. Mastery experience builds confidence, as past success makes an individual feel like achievement can be repeated. Vicarious experience contributes, as well; efficacious people have seen success in action modeled for them. Typically supported people, individuals with high self-efficacy receive verbal persuasion from respected social connections.

Interestingly, a person's emotional state also contributes to efficacy. Stress researchers have empirically proven that fear, stress, and anxiety set off hormonal chain reactions in the body that elevate blood cortisol and adrenaline. This response limits upper-level cognition, impairs physiology, and reduces feelings of efficacy. A person with high self-efficacy typically knows how to manage their stress. Numerous studies validate self-efficacy as a tool to promote positive health behaviors, and cultivating efficacy has been found to build traits that define resilience.

Researchers repeatedly found in numbers both practically and statistically significant that the ability to self-correct, demonstrate confidence, and exude sociability helped individuals thrive despite dire circumstances and trauma histories. By 1995, researchers had clearly demonstrated a case for the existence of key, identifiable traits that made a person resilient. The question moving forward became not whether resilience was real, but whether it could be cultivated.

Put simply, people can train themselves to be resilient for those times when hardship comes unexpectedly. Controlled pressure followed by specific exercises to de-escalate the body's reaction creates the ability to handle more pressure next time. Cultivation is core to the theory's concept; the resiliency model was developed to highlight the process whereby an individual moves through stages of biopsychospiritual (holistic, whole-person) homeostasis. Simple studies have consistently highlighted the model's central premise, that disruption followed by time and self-care aimed at reintegration actually cultivates resilient traits.

A story I often share with my students is a hard one to hear for those of us who are animal lovers, but it paints vividly the concept of resilience cultivation. In this noteworthy demonstration endeavor, researchers used baby chickens to make the point that resilience is something we can learn through experience.

Painting the chicks and grouping them in separate pens, the first group was left alone to interact happily and normally. The second group was periodically picked up and stressed in a confined space. After the stress, the chick was given time back in their group pen to recuperate. The third group was continually stressed in the confined space, with no recovery time or play opportunity with other chickens. The researchers created three distinct populations with different experiences.

After raising them for a time in this manner, all the painted chicks were placed in buckets of water, with researchers timing their struggle until drowning. *I know, this sounds just awful.* It doesn't have a happy ending but there is an interesting lesson, I promise.

The chicks that had been continually stressed drowned almost immediately; they had no hope in the face of hardship that they could swim. The second group to succumb was comprised of those "happy innocents" in group one who had never been confined and stressed. They didn't know how to withstand this watery hardship and folded in the face of it. The last swimmers fighting to make it were the chicks from the stress adaptation group. Somehow, the confinement stressors followed by time to recover had rendered them stronger and able to swim and survive much longer than their peers. This group was resilient; they had experienced hardship before and believed they had a chance to make it and recover. They had those past mastery experiences to rely on, and they just fought to keep swimming.[6]

Researchers interested in psychological and social determinants of health picked up the concept of resilience and have gradually extended its use from the domain of mental health to health in general. Early work on resilience was concerned with the individual, but more recently researchers have become interested in resilience as a feature of whole communities. Resilient traits can be taught, but this does not happen in a vacuum. Cultural analysis to ensure applicability is vital.

Such cultural consideration defines modern Resiliency Theory; this third wave builds upon existing ecological theory work in health promotion to consider the multiple layers that impact us as individuals. Ecological theories explain the way that the push and pull of one's environment yields tremendous influence on choices and behaviors. Third-wave Resiliency Theory works to apply questions of environment and culture to any study of individual resilient traits, with the goal being more effective cultivation of those traits by focusing on building them within supportive communities invested in doing the same. This wave is influenced by postmodern, multidisciplinary efforts to identify motivational forces both in individuals, groups, and larger communities while simultaneously analyzing context and group experience.

That sounds nerdy and complicated, but it really just means that the theory is about looking to maximize assets people already have within them in every space they exist, socially interact, and work.

Resiliency Theory as it applies to health behavior change is a powerful paradigm from which to approach research and programming, primarily because it promotes a model of agency and client control. Research has shown that, indeed, much of what seems to promote positive adaptation despite adversity does originate outside of the individual—in the family, the community, the society, the culture, and the environment. A confrontation with adversity can lead to a new level of growth, indicating that resilience is something innate that needs only to be properly awakened.

The Resilient Veteran

Trying to help military veterans using this theory involves asking them to get involved in their own healing process. It actively discourages victim identities and speaks to warrior culture much differently than the highly stigmatized clinical intervention model does. Well-known theorist Dr. Richardson wrote of this difference, "the health education and prevention professions are in the midst of a philosophical revolution attempting to build upon negative risk reduction programs, which are driven by the medical model, to competency models."[7] As discussed extensively in the previous chapter, particularly in marginalized or insular communities, capacity assessments emphasizing positive assets can be powerful.

Applying Resiliency Theory to the military has yielded positive results to date. Post service, some individuals are more psychologically resilient when faced with reintegration stresses, and we can help train everyone to that standard. For those who struggle with resilience the way I did, increasing understanding of resilience within given communities and populations may help target programming that offers an alternative to the lonely six-pack of beer.

For example, one 2010 pilot study of returning National Guard soldiers completing their deployment to Iraq demonstrated that high levels of resilient characteristics fully mediated the likelihood of self-reported depressive symptoms. If soldiers were categorized as having resilient traits, they did not also report mental health issues.

Another study found the same protective effects offered by resilient adaptability in 2013. This Canadian study assessed the criterion validity of a model of psychological resilience composed of various intrapersonal and interpersonal variables for predicting mental health among Canadian Forces (CF) members returning from overseas deployment. Participants included 1,584 male CF members who were deployed in support of the mission in Afghanistan between 2008 and 2010. The results demonstrated the importance of resilient traits in predicting better mental health in Canadian veterans and emphasized the protective nature of conscientiousness, emotional stability, and positive social interactions. The more prominent traits indicating resilience that a soldier held, the better their mental health after returning from combat.[8]

Helping Veterans Experience Reintegration Characterized by Resilience

This section could also be titled, Don't Do What I Did.

The process of psychological reintegration is the ability to learn new skills from the disruptive experience and put life's perspective back in a way that will increase abilities to negotiate life events. Serving in the military (whether one went to war or remained in garrison) is a significant disruption to life in an era where so few Americans do so. Military personnel are a minority, and during the return to civilian life they are faced with disruptive stressors socially, professionally, mentally, and emotionally.

To optimally reach veterans struggling with transition requires reaching out to teach resilience well before that transition begins. There is value in learning to manage stress, hardship, and challenge, and buttressing specific areas of our lives can do that. The challenge for health professionals looking to stem the tide of service suicides and improve quality of life for veterans lies in shifting the paradigm away from a focus on problems and toward theories and methods of resiliency cultivation, preparation, and self-care practices.

Resiliency Theory outlines three key areas of focus: social support, self-care endeavors, and faith practices, which will be discussed in detail in the successive three chapters of this book. There are specific techniques that can help both veterans and active duty personnel raise their own levels of resilience, and all of them can be taught and assessed as performance metrics.

The Department of Defense has begun to see the validity of such behavioral health interventions in Wounded Warrior recovery programs aimed to treat service members with existing cases of depression and is constantly and creatively expanding research partnerships to validate such treatment methods. Some of the research efforts are explicitly clinical and apply rigorous prospective, mixed-methods models. For example, a recent study in the District of Columbia in partnership with the DC Veteran's Hospital, American University's Psychology Department, and the War-Related Illness and Injury Study Center (WRIISC) yielded promising treatment results for mindfulness meditation interventions.[9]

While it is tremendously exciting that we are starting to see the value of such piecemeal programs to treat people already struggling, my hope is that we can take another step to insert protective trait training into the active duty world. We can make things better for those who come after us with some savvy programs based on good evaluation evidence.

Both cultural analysis and examination of ecologically focused Resiliency Theory suggest that the ways health promoters bring programs to veterans must emphasize assets and agency. Three decades of evidence provides us with a road map to success: the best method for building resilience is to learn and regularly employ techniques to improve social support, self-care, and spirituality.

***

Her journey to health and wholeness wasn't a quick one, nor was it handed to her in a prescription pill, but Sarah worked her way into resilience and healing. She became a yoga teacher and nutrition nut and started praying a whole lot more. Once, she made me eat a red hamburger made entirely out of beets.

It was awful, but I loved what she was trying to teach me.

Today she gives speeches about sexual assault and healing trauma, focusing heavily on the role of individual agency in recovery. She teaches yoga to other veterans today, always making her classes free and accessible for those who might find the mat to be the useful alternative that she did. Shifting her wistful gaze away from the pistol required choice. Replacing unhealthy behaviors with healthier ones involved many changes, and choosing to work and spend time with a trusted tribe of affirming people who valued the same things she did gave her a chance to move forward.

If you ask her, she will tell you that she'd change none of it.

When I think of her, I know this old expression to be true: beautiful people aren't born; they're made.

Chapter 6

FINDING A TRIBE:
THE IMPORTANCE OF SOCIAL SUPPORT

The last decade of war has affected the relationship between our society and the military. As a nation, we've learned to separate the warrior from the war. But we still have much to learn about how to connect the warrior to the citizen. . . . We can't allow a sense of separation to grow between us.[1]

—Gen. Martin Dempsey, chairman of the Joint Chiefs of Staff, 2013

Blayne Smith came home from Iraq after spending almost a year there in 2004. He was a lieutenant in the First Cavalry Division, leading a scout platoon in the lawless region between Baghdad and Fallujah.

His guys ran over two hundred combat missions during their deployment, and their accomplishments were many: they'd captured insurgents on the Black List, uncovered caches of weapons, and made things harder for an enemy constantly trying to send rocket and mortar attacks into both cities.

Blayne loved leading soldiers, and despite the daily stress, the bombs that turned vehicles and humans into charcoal and rain, and the weight of decisions made that he knew would irrevocably change lives, he was fulfilled. They had close calls, but everyone made it home. Smith loved his soldiers, his job, and knew he wanted to stay in the Army.

Coming home, he wasn't the same person who had packed and repacked his bags ten months previously. His fuse seemed shorter, but he dismissed it and no one really seemed to mind too much. Blayne wanted to keep serving, and he joined the Special Forces (SF) to see if he could contribute even more next time he went overseas. In truth, he had been amazed by the SF guys he had seen in Iraq. In urban combat, Army Special Forces soldiers were fluid, confident, and decisive. They spoke Arabic. Mostly, they knew what they were doing—when they kicked in a door, the bad guys were often inside.

SF guys will say that they're like brothers, but that's just a word civilians can understand, and it's the best the guys can do to explain something indescribable. After nearly two years of training together, Smith's team of twelve was tight. During the week, they ran, rucked, and did CrossFit workouts. On weekends, they barbequed around the pool with their wives, kids, and girlfriends. They pushed each other even at events like this and always competed to see who had the best backflip. They spent weeks on training missions living crammed like cordwood in the equivalent of a doublewide trailer.

Smith's guys will tell you that he led from the front, that he never asked them to do something he wouldn't do, and that he appealed to their desire to be the best. They'll also tell you that because Smith was fast, strong, and a great shot, he set a bar everyone wanted to beat. They drove each other to be faster, stronger, and more accurate because they all wanted to be the number-one guy.

The ribbing was good natured but was as relentless as the competition. They teased slow runners without mercy, like their senior medic, Marc. They came up with many clever barbs and said he had one speed, whether there was a soccer ball in front of him or a lion behind him. The team knew what made each other tick, and what ticked each other off. Their confidence in each other was absolute.

It became a bond impossible to explain.

It wasn't long before another deployment called, this time to Afghanistan. At the time, Blayne and his wife, Megan, had a two-year-old son and Megan was expecting their second. Blayne had a feeling that things would be serious this deployment, and he got busy making a spreadsheet of all the household bills and getting things organized around their house. He couldn't tell Megan exactly where he was heading, but he didn't have to share with her the reasons for his preparations or the risks ahead; she knew those all too well.

His team wound up at Firebase Anaconda in southern Afghanistan. It was nothing fancy, just a tiny outpost in a hotly contested remote river valley. At least twice, Taliban fighters had descended from the mountains and tried to overwhelm the base. Whenever a convoy left its walls, an attack by the enemy was expected.

One rainy and cold day, their team was leaving a meeting in a nearby village when they picked up radio chatter. They all knew what *"Do you want me to do work on the Americans?"* meant, and a second later bullets began snapping and the ground exploded. Smith raced to the front seat of his vehicle to radio for air support while the gunner let loose with the M240. Blayne looked up at his driver, who had turned and was shouting something at him that he couldn't hear, at first.

Marc had been shot in the face.

Smith left the cover of his HMMWV and sprinted the 150 meters toward Marc's truck, his feet slipping in the mud as rounds plunged into the ground around him. When he reached it, he saw Marc lying perfectly still on his back, with the junior medic working feverishly over him. Smith had expected to see Marc hunched over, holding a bleeding wound, expected to tell him to get his ass in the truck. But Marc wasn't blinking, and there wasn't much blood. His beard and scarf hid the entry point of the bullet, near his chin.

Later that night, Smith cried in front of his team. He couldn't help it. They all cried. Everyone loved Marc, their one-speed running companion, a gregarious, hilarious guy, and an avid Phillies and Eagles fan with a fiancé back home.

There were still missions to run, and they were back at it the next day. Eight days later, Smith's truck led a convoy of five vehicles going about 10 miles per hour along a narrow track cut into a terraced hillside. To their left, the ground sloped sharply to the river below.

The attack started all at once as the enormous boom of a rocket-propelled grenade sounded behind Smith and destroyed the rock wall on his right.

Machine gun fire erupted from the river and a panicked voice came over the radio: *Truck three is destroyed. Truck three is completely destroyed!*

Truck three had been hit by a remote-detonated bomb that flipped it over and blew the turret gunner nearly thirty feet into the air.

He spun like a rag doll and landed hard, shattering his right leg and injuring his back. The medic, Linsey, ran through small-arms fire to drag him away from the raging fireball as ammunition and explosives began cooking off in all directions.

Linsey next found their team sergeant, Dave, on his hands and knees behind the burning wreck; from the passenger seat he'd been blown free of the vehicle, but he'd been caught in the flash. His boots and flame-retardant uniform were mostly intact, but he was badly burned.

Linsey bent down, and through the roar of ammunition asked if he could walk. Unable to talk, Dave nodded, and the 160-pound medic guided his 230-plus team sergeant through Taliban AK-47 and machine gun rounds to the truck and put an IV in his foot. Dave would die later that night.

The firefight was deafening. The smell of gunpowder, diesel fumes, and iron filled the air. The team's Afghan interpreter, Eman, had also been thrown clear, but lay dead with barely a scrape on him. Tim, the Air Force combat controller who had been working with them, landed about forty feet uphill of the truck. The force had blown his kit off, and the springs that fed ammunition up through the magazines in the pouches were sticking out—all 210 rounds had exploded. As air support provided cover, Smith collected the remains of Tim's broken body and placed them all together on the stretcher.

Smith found Jeremy, truck three's driver, last. He'd been pinned inside the burning truck, and by the time they got to him he was nearly unrecognizable. While one of his teammates lifted the flaming mass with a pry bar, Smith, wearing a pair of asbestos mittens, carefully pulled the soldier free. The two men carried their friend to a waiting truck in a tarp.

And then he went home, back to sunny Florida where ambushes weren't a daily worry.

Smith left the Army in January 2010 and moved his family to Tampa where his days soon fell into a rhythm. He would help Megan get the boys off to school, put on his blue-striped shirt and red tie, pull out of the driveway of his 3,000-square-foot home in the gated community where no one cut his own grass, and drive his Toyota Camry past the old people playing golf.

He would get about two miles down the road before the tape in his head began to play: *You did everything you could. There wasn't more you could have done. Well, maybe. It was raining. We should have cancelled that day. What would a day have meant?*

Then the reel of grief and guilt and shame would skip: *Maybe I just need to quit my job and join the National Guard. Work for the CIA or the FBI. Maybe if I worked in defense or intel, that will make everything better.*

And skip again: *Why do I keep having this conversation? Why can't I be happy with what I have? What kind of idiot am I that I can't be happy with this life?*

Over and over and over it played.

As a medical sales guy, Smith made good money now, but all it brought was shame. He'd look around at all the expensive, useless stuff in their nice home and fantasize about giving it all away and raising his family on $800 a month.

He couldn't enjoy his life and he couldn't be happy about being out of the Army. He'd planned all along—before any of that awful stuff in Afghanistan happened—to leave the Army when he did. But instead of being happy about finally being home for good with Megan and the boys, he felt like a failure.

Smith's Army career had spanned twelve years. He felt like his last act of that career was to get part of his team blown up. And whether it was true or not, it felt like he had run away. And now he had a job with no purpose, no obligation to the greater good, and he just wasn't prepared for what stuff like that would do to a guy like him.

I failed, then quit.

At home, he spent long hours in his office, often unable to close his laptop, open the door, and hang out with his family. If one of the kids barged in, Smith turned on Megan: *Can't you see I'm trying to make a living here?*

He couldn't tolerate the daily hassles—packing lunches, planning dinners. It is hard to see the importance of things like that when you've spent so long trying to keep people safe. When you've watched your friends die.

New to Tampa, he didn't bother making friends. He didn't have much in common with most and it didn't seem worth the effort. When people found out what he did in the Army they asked too many questions or said things that made him cringe: *You're Special Forces? You must be such a tough guy.*

Megan had never seen someone so unhappy. Her husband had quit doing everything that had once brought him joy. The tires on his mountain bike went flat. The soles of his golf and soccer shoes rotted. His guitar sat silent and out of tune. She tried to help—took stuff with the kids and the house off his plate, fixed up his mountain bike for Father's Day, bought him a golf membership. He rode the bike once and used the membership twice.

She kept waiting for the person she knew to come back. In all the years she'd known him, Smith had never once raised his voice. But his reactions were unfamiliar, unpredictable now.

His anger flared and his tone had changed—it was impatient, frustrated, exasperated. No matter what she and the boys did, it felt wrong. She was finally starting up her own career, but instead of support, Smith lobbed criticism of pretty much everything—her employer, her hours, her pay.

Blayne wasn't sure why his family relationships were becoming so difficult, he just knew that they were. When his oldest son—a sweetly awkward, precocious kid who taught his mom to play chess when he was three—talked back at the dinner table, it sent Smith into a rage. He never raised a hand to the boy, but he let him have it. Smith whacked the hard surface with the flat of his hand hard enough to make the silverware jump.[2]

***

At the time, he would never have voluntarily labeled himself as struggling, but stress injury like Blayne's creates numbness and emotional reactivity that get in the way of family bonds and close friendships. For so many veterans, this exacerbates reconnection issues with family and friends after service.[3]

As discussed in chapter 3, social support is vital to mental wellness because it lowers stress levels. It is natural and adaptive for humans to seek connection with one another, and interruptions to those close connections are uniquely traumatizing. Loneliness and rejection feel like threats to life and future stability to our nervous systems, and the result is measurable impact on physical health. Strained social relationships only increase the reactivity in a person already struggling with stress injury.

Scientists have studied social support from a variety of angles, looking at the size of networks, whether or not someone has a confidante, partnership status, and the perceived quality of support received. Having a trusted tribe is good for you. Research examples abound.[4] In one study, medical students who were lonely had depressed immune systems. In another, unmarried cancer patients died at greater rates than married peers with the disease. Even elderly dementia patients with more friends stayed sharper longer than their lonelier peers.

Social support is a known contributor to health and longevity, with recent studies indicating that high levels add 7.5 years to the average American lifespan. Researchers didn't always talk about social support and the vital role it plays in our ability to grow through traumas. In fact, the first study on this phenomenon happened by accident at a medical conference, when a Midwestern college professor met a local physician in a pub.

The researcher's name was Dr. Stuart Wolf, and he spent his time studying the alarming rate at which heart attacks were on the rise in 1950s America. His new acquaintance listened with interest to his talk of lifestyle-created heart disease and offered him an opportunity that sounded strange. He suggested that Dr. Wolf visit his hometown, a small village in Pennsylvania called Roseto. He had been a physician there his whole life and never seen the heart attacks Dr. Wolf was describing.

Curious, Dr. Wolf visited and found that the small-town physician had been right—people were simply not dying of heart attacks in Roseto. Dr. Wolf would spend the next three decades studying town citizens to find out why.

Although the Italian immigrants who inhabited the town of Roseto drank wine, cooked with lard, and struggled with obesity, they were remarkably healthy and boasted above-average lifespans. Their secret was in their social cohesion. The townspeople lived in nuclear families and interacted with extended family members throughout their lives. They didn't live in idyllic harmony, but they were closely connected to one another. They supported one another emotionally, and there was always a neighbor to help a parent keep an unruly child in line. The community was homogeneous and close, living in extended kinship networks that kept families near one another and allowed the elderly to age in the same home as their grandchildren.

Before future generations moved to the suburbs and increased their work hours, divorce rates, and stress in their lives, the rates of heart disease within this community lay exponentially below national averages, though lifestyle behaviors were far from heart healthy. The primary difference noted among the first and second generation of study participants was the uniquely warm and cohesive community relationships typical in the small town for first generation inhabitants.

Dr. Wolfs' thirty-year study highlighted the vital importance of close, nurturing relationships to human health and what came to be known as the "Roseto Effect." Social support can improve anyone's life, but studies have shown that specifically in military settings, high levels of perceived social support independently predict coping self-efficacy post-deployment.[5]

***

Sometimes he thought it was crazy, driving for a half hour to meet Mike Erwin at 5:30 a.m., running with him for an hour, then driving thirty minutes back home again. But when Erwin came to Tampa the summer after Smith separated from the Army and asked if he wanted to train for a marathon and raise money for wounded vets, Smith jumped at the chance.

For the vets?

Of course.

So over the hottest summer on record, when the dew point was so high they had to turn their windshield wipers on in the morning, Smith and Erwin trained together. Four times a week, they met in the dark on Bayshore Boulevard, the four and a half-mile stretch of sidewalk that hugs Hillsborough Bay in South Tampa.

As they trained on those humid mornings, they found space to talk with one another. They talked about leadership, accountability, family. And they talked shop. Erwin had been part of Smith's unit, a task force intelligence officer in Kandahar. He'd heard Smith's calls come in over the radio, and those two days haunted him too. He knew what kept Smith up at night.

"You did the best you could," he told Blayne.

They ran until the sun came up, until they could wring streams of water from their shirts. They stretched and drank Gatorade in the parking lot and talked about bottling that endorphin rush and post-hard run feeling. They were soaked and spent and felt amazing.

Erwin left in August and Smith kept running. He allowed himself this one thing because training for the race wasn't about him. It was about the vets and the money they would raise for Wounded Warriors. He was committed to the cause and so he ran. He often left his music at home and just thought about stuff on long runs that were so humid his sweat turned his shoes to squeegees..

For two, three hours, he wondered: *Why do I feel so bad? Am I doing a bad job as a dad? What am I supposed to be doing with my life?*

After he ran, he felt better.

That fall, he met up with Army buddies he hadn't seen in nearly a year, and together they ran the Twin Cities Marathon with Team Red, White, and Blue. It was a small team at the time, something Mike had started talking about getting going to help connect veterans to one another and their local communities through fitness. Smith finished in 3:50, went home, and kept running. He'd been lurching around for so long looking for something that made him feel better, and he felt like he had finally found it doing these group races and raising money for charity. Smith felt like running to help out wounded guys might be something he could anchor himself to.

It was during his next marathon that the light bulb finally went on. He and Erwin were talking about all the guys they knew who weren't doing that well at present. They had so many friends who were struggling with being civilians—guys who got out of the service who wanted back in, guys who felt lost on the outside, unhappy and directionless, guys who were joining Team RWB not because they wanted to help other vets, but because they needed to help. To belong to something. To reach for something. To give back.

Damn it. That's me.

When things were at their darkest, after Megan had told him they were through, Smith started writing down three good things that happened to him every day. Without fail, most of his entries came from what he saw on his runs along Bayshore. He'd write about dolphins rolling in the bay, pelicans dive-bombing for fish, the way the Tampa skyline looked so pretty at sunrise. Back then, after he promised Megan he would do anything to make things right, after he started seeing a counselor at the Veterans Administration, after he moved out, he ran all the time. He couldn't eat, he couldn't sleep, and his gut burned. He felt like he was living someone else's life, and he just needed to run the horror of it out of him with people who understood.

After they separated, his nights suddenly yawned with the emptiness of a quiet house, and so one Tuesday he forced himself to go to a run club hosted by a local Irish pub.

I need to make some friends.

So he showed up, ran a 5-K, and started talking to a few guys. They told him about another club on Thursdays. Pretty soon, he was a regular at both and scheduling the rest of his life around those two runs.

He didn't need other runners to push him—he needed their friendship.

For Smith, much has come to pass: he left the Army, but not his fellow veterans. After Megan's words convinced him to get help, he made the choice to leave his sales job to enter the nonprofit sector. The purpose he was hoping for in his work he found by becoming the Team Red, White, and Blue nonprofit's first employee.

None of it was easy, but finally seeing a counselor helped him forgive himself, and running with other veterans helped him wade back into civilian life. He knows now that he did what he thought was right in Afghanistan, and his shame has subsided. He is a leader again, helping guide and mentor veterans, easing their transition home, creating programs that keep them active and challenged, and turning soldiers into athletes. It tempers the last of the grief and the guilt.

And so now, finally, there is room for joy. For patience and laughter, fun with his boys, work that brings him joy, and even new love.

***

Today, Blayne is the executive director of the nonprofit Team Red, White, and Blue. The group works specifically to help veterans struggling the way he once was, though you'd be hard pressed to ever get him to use that word. TeamRWB works to connect veterans to their civilian community and draws them in by appealing to their interests in community service, physical fitness, and social interaction with other veterans.

The group asks civilian community members not for financial support or cheerful words, but for their time. RWB brings two divided communities together around shared interests of fitness and fun activities, many of them designed for families. By creating regular, healthy spaces for veterans to connect with one another and with civilians who are willing to spend their time in like ways, the organization cultivates new chances for social cohesion.[6]

***

Not all veterans lose their social support systems upon returning home, though many of us do. It can be tough to stay close to people when we aren't sure that we speak the same language any longer.

Some veterans are blessed with the ability to keep communication lines open, even in hard times and with loved ones able to weather the storm alongside. These are the cases that highlight even more powerfully the importance of connection, and I will always be grateful that this was my brother's experience.

I was already deployed to Iraq when my brother e-mailed me to share that he was probably going to propose to his girlfriend before he headed over. She was a civilian schoolteacher from Philadelphia that I had yet to meet, and I just rolled my eyes when he shared his romantic plans with me. I was surrounded by guys losing their girlfriends to the grind of deployment, and I expected that his schoolteacher would be mailing him the same "Dear John" letter after a few months. I told him I didn't have a problem with the proposal but admonished him to buy her a ring made out of cubic zirconia. No sense in buying a diamond he might never get back.

As younger brothers often do, he ignored my advice and bought her a beautiful ring.

Well, that is some cash he will never see again! Should have listened to me!

When a wounded service member is medically evacuated, he or she often has a long period in a hospital ward and in lots of different outpatient treatment facilities ahead. There are no guarantees and it is painful for both the patient and those standing alongside. I watched the prospect of a long, uncertain recovery level some people. In others, I watched uncertainty and trauma bring out their diamond-hard character.

When my brother arrived at Bethesda, we didn't know what he might be facing. There was so much damage. On his third surgery, the physicians in the operating room took a vote about whether or not to amputate his leg at the hip; he had infection setting in and they were worried it could get worse. Two voted to amputate, and three voted to give him a couple of days.

Ward 5 was a dark place some days. We were surrounded by morphine drips, pain, injury, and struggling families who weren't sure what to make of it all.

Into this world walked my brother's civilian schoolteacher.

She won't be able to handle this.

Throughout this period I watched his young fiancé with a cynical eye. I stereotyped her on sight—she was a pretty girl who often wore makeup and always had on matching accessories. I assumed she lacked gravitas and would fall apart any minute.

She never did.

When her leave ran out at work she went back to teaching all day long in nearby Virginia, but made the drive every night to sleep in a chair at my brother's bedside. I would find her sitting by his side laughing about some silly thing or another, always keeping him smiling. She never complained and never gave up, never confessed fears about marrying a man with so many new health issues.

While I fumbled gracelessly in his hospital room, once even dropping a portable DVD player on his gaping wounds, she was all kindness and poise. She kept him looking toward their future on a daily basis. Even when he left the hospital and had to spend long days in a reclining chair. Even when he needed help with any and all of the most basic tasks.

The makeup had fooled me; she was more than serious. Only in her twenties, she helped him make it to the bathroom, shower, move, and get through hard physical therapy appointments without complaint. I don't think I ever saw her with messy hair either.

There were guys on the ward whose wives filed for divorce when they saw what they were going to have to struggle through together. I don't think the thought ever crossed her mind.

She helped him through medical retirement, a search for a new career and a civilian identity, and they became parents with that joyous excitement reserved for newbies who don't yet know how much sleep they will soon go without.

She married a Marine with three sisters, all of whom would gladly hide a body for her today—no questions asked.

She has a good memory though. Every now and again, I hear about that cubic zirconia comment.

Chapter 7

SELF-CARE AND MENTAL FITNESS TRAINING

She left the wire before the sun was up with her platoon of combat engineers, focused on erecting barriers around several Iraqi polling sites for the next day's elections. The teams moved fast, and while they worked they were alert for the IED attacks they knew could happen at any moment. The sun beat down on them and in their body armor, 103 degree-heat felt like more.

By the time she closed her eyes that night, she had thrown up six times.

Theresa Larson was a lot of things. She had been a college athlete, a fitness competitor, and she was now an Officer of Marines in Al Anbar. She struggled with bulimia, but that was not part of her public story. Her intensity and competitive spirit had always made her hard on herself—the combat environment simply turned it up and sharpened her edges to razors.

Always one to push herself on the sports field, she loved to do something anyone doubted she could. She was the youngest sister of athletic older brothers always striving to keep up, which is one of many reasons she wound up in the Marine Corps. The other reasons were similar to the Marines in body armor all around her—she wanted to serve in a way that meant getting her hands dirty, to make a difference in the world around her, and to be the fittest, toughest Marine Officer she could in the process.

You okay, Lieutenant?
Hell yes, Marine.
What is okay?

***

Self-care is a word in vogue today, but few people actually practice it. We live amidst an epidemic of chronic overstimulation and tend to embrace treatment of the health issues that come along with that rather than do the harder, slower work of bringing our nervous systems back into a regulated state.

Self-care doesn't mean exercising until ibuprofen is your best friend. However, when it came to my physical health, this was a mistake I made for years. In general, I was always wired and rarely stopped moving, but I thought that simply meant I was working hard enough. I thought that *pain was weakness leaving the body* and more intensity was always a good thing for my athletic abilities.

Pain breeds strength, right? I'd better push it harder . . .

I loved fitness and went back to school to study exercise science. After studying performance physiology for the briefest of times, anyone can quickly learn how false these ideas about overtraining as virtue are. I kept at it, however.

I'm a slow learner. I had to figure it out in an emergency room.

I could write an entire book about the optimal way to practice physical self-care,[1] and many smarter than me have done so. The bottom line is that designing a care plan centered around a principle of balance is vital. Combining keen self-awareness with intensity and self-discipline yields the best results for any athlete, of any level.

***

I spent a few years in the hilly areas of central Virginia dedicating at least five days each week to running. I always ran with a stopwatch to make sure I logged more than thirty minutes. I would get truly irritated with myself if I skipped a run. I did distance races now and again, often unable to walk normally for weeks afterward. My first marathon was particularly crippling; I pulled something in a hip (who knows what because I never went to a doctor) and just tried to rest it for a few days and then get right to my punishing routine.

Pain is weakness.

I was amazed at what happened to my body composition and fitness performance when I stopped running those marathons and half marathons. As with most changes of this nature, it didn't happen because I listened to someone savvier about training than me; it was something I stumbled into one winter. I spent a freezing few months in Minnesota and moved all my training indoors out of necessity.

I had to get creative since I couldn't run in those waist-deep snowdrifts, and I started having fun with it. I stayed really active, but started moving my body in different ways. I joined one of those fancy gyms that are more like an adult playground than a fitness facility. I had access to everything from a swimming pool to a tanning bed. (I'm Irish and Norwegian and unfortunately, I left Minnesota looking like I had been living in the Bahamas. I'd place bets that in the future I will pay dearly for that carelessness at the dermatologist's office).

Some of the stuff I tried felt not only new but surprisingly challenging, which was exactly the point. One morning, I was huffing and puffing my way through a deep-water aerobics class trying not to let the elderly woman next to me see how hard I was working. They had sweetly and quite deceptively talked me into strapping floats onto my ankles and carrying a set of foam dumbbells. In the water both made me feel like I was dying after ten minutes. That season, I tried everything from dance aerobics to circuit weight training. Some of my workouts were longer, some really short. They were all different and some felt kind of weird. I embarrassed myself in the dance classes, usually, but pretty soon, pain wasn't an ever-present force in my daily life.

When I returned to my warmer home climate, I was amazed that all my run times had improved, even on hills. I'd dropped a bit of body fat and hadn't been trying to. I felt relaxed and calm.

Of course, I got right back into my running shoes, and I was still proud of those runs that were so fast I threw up at the end.

When we talk about caring for our physical body, we often emphasize movement, movement, off the couch! In actuality, balance is one of the most important things a person can plan into a training calendar. The physical practices that offer us stress reduction and a return to homeostatic balance are beneficial in a myriad of ways. It cannot be all about raising our heart rate and shrinking a derriere. Those things are fine, but balanced physical self-care with a keen focus on regulating an overstimulated nervous system must become priorities to anyone looking to cultivate resilience.

Here's the good news: there is more than one way to do this. You have the freedom to figure out which activities work best for your personality, resources, and preferences. It is beyond the scope of this small book to outline every health practice available to promote a resilient physical state, and I will endeavor simply to share the merit of self-care in whatever form feels most appealing to the individual.

Trying out mindful movement practices and learning from the pros who teach them is my favorite hobby. For me, the most relaxing physical practice available changes based on what's happening in my life. There have been times when the answer was trail running, yoga, swimming, or rowing. The fun part is trying new options out with an eye toward what you should be feeling if it is a practice that is bringing you into balance. Healthy practices are not abusive. When it is a balancing activity, you'll feel yourself exerting but peaceful. You will sleep a bit better. You may notice your mind slow down a bit. You may pay attention to your body in a new way.

Hey! I just noticed how much tighter my left hip is than my right! I wonder if I should spend some time stretching that side more?

Self-care of this sort also provides mental fitness training that can hone focus, improve performance, and increase resilience. Remember the last group of swimming chicks? They succeeded because they had been exposed to challenge followed by recovery. Such training involves purposeful movement that brings attentive focus to the physical body and the racing mind. This attention trains the body in both challenging and balanced fashion, while carving in space for activation of the parasympathetic nervous system. It is here that the body restores, improves, and hormone levels in the blood go back to their optimal levels. Balanced training pushes your envelope and then sets the reset button!

Mindful movement is a unique way to build mental toughness; it creates opportunities for mastery experience and a platform from which to build physical stability. Interestingly, most of us are not physically stable without very intentionally working to become so. We sit too much, slouch a bit, and create muscular imbalances that we don't notice because we often zip through our days without paying attention to present-tense sensations in our tissues.

We all live in an obesogenic environment where it is easier to find fast food than fresh vegetables, and we are all constantly overstimulated. It is easy to dismiss just how stimulating our environments typically are because we get used to an unhealthy norm. That cell phone is really not supposed to be next to your pillow at night. Come on, we can at least admit that level of overstimulation is not normal, right?

I recall sitting with a friend in a shopping mall a few years ago. We sat down at a little table near the food court and were trying to chat and catch up a bit while she snuggled her toddler in her lap. We were surrounded by flat-screen televisions that were all blaring different stations to entertain food court patrons. Her little boy looked around in alarm, then buried his face in her shoulder and started weeping.

I felt like joining him. His young system wasn't used to blaring techno-noise and his reaction to the shrillness was to retreat to his mom. I remember thinking that he was setting an example for the adults in the room who had all gotten used to ten television sets blaring overhead while they ate a rushed meal of fast food. This is not normal for our physical bodies!

The pace of modern life is frenetic. Our bodies read this "go, go, go" message clearly, and stress embeds itself in our minds and bodies.

As discussed in chapter 3, the stress response is a completely natural phenomenon, and the human body operates intelligently to produce appropriate reactions to life's surprises. Upon registering some sort of threat, the brain sends hormonal signals to the adrenal glands, which secrete cortisol and adrenaline to empower the body to handle it. In a healthy negative feedback system, the cortisol signals the hypothalamus to shut down the response, provided the threat has disappeared. This stress response happens at an intensity level in relation to the threat. It is instructive and animal, and is necessary for performance, self-preservation, and survival.

Everyone's response to stimuli differs, and what is stimulating to one person biochemically may not be to another. That doesn't mean our systems aren't registering the stimulation, however. Ten televisions keep my nervous system on the alert, even if I don't view them as threatening in the same way that my friend's toddler did.

The problem with the human stress response does not become apparent until the stress becomes chronic, and the bloodstream contains too much cortisol. Chronic stress occurs when the brain's hypothalamus refuses to shut off the chemical signals it is sending, because it still perceives a problem. In our modern society with constantly ringing phones, troubled interpersonal relationships, and an ever-increasing pace enabled by technology, chronic stress is rampant.

When the body's stress response is constantly firing, blood cortisol levels are too high and inflammatory proteins become more present in the bloodstream. A host of illnesses and inflammatory conditions have been related to this chemical imbalance. The body's immune system becomes overactive and confused by the aberrant proteins. Unsure what foreign bodies to attack, autoimmune illnesses like rheumatoid arthritis and allergies become real health issues. Unchecked, unacknowledged stress is a killer in too many ways to count. Chronic stress has been linked to a host of physical maladies including: abdominal weight gain, cancer, gastrointestinal illnesses, depression, and chronic pain.[2]

We can't always prevent surprises that send our bodies into reaction mode, but we can prepare them for stress and adopt a positive outlook toward challenge, in general. This concept of mind-set will be discussed in the final chapter of this book so that we can focus here specifically on physical self-care practices that build resilience to stressors. Consider self-care preventive training, because it truly is!

***

Theresa had always struggled with low points that she never labeled depression, but her eating disorder had never been as bad as that summer in Iraq. She was dizzy, spacey, and knew she needed to find a balance to keep moving forward safely.

She would do anything to protect her Marines, but she didn't know how to extend that kindness to herself. The voices that screamed hostilities when she looked in the mirror were getting louder, and she knew she needed to make a change.

How could she be an athlete and a competitor without abusing her physical body?

There had to be a new way to think about things.

That was her beginning.

***

Health is a term commercially co-opted. Rarely do we discuss healthy practices as interrelated, highly personalized techniques for bringing base-level balance to a person. We often talk about ideal aesthetics or extreme performance instead.

Because I liked training, for a little while I worked in the fitness industry as a teacher and trainer. I thought it would be mostly about helping people feel empowered, but I felt like I was too often having conversations about weight loss and fitting into a desired jeans size. Sometimes the people who focused most heavily on working with me for these reasons were the most likely to skip sessions or to tell me they had splurged at McDonald's the day prior.

We need to care about something deeper to change behavior.

The sorts of practices that create bodily strength and balance are very different from those touted to meet an appearance metric. These focused practices are not additional stressors on the body but rather provide physical buttress and support that both regulate the nervous system and build resilience. Training still means pushing the envelope to promote growth, but the ways in which most of us were taught to do that are contraindicated and less than helpful.

Self-care means embracing a focus on holistic health, on prioritizing the physical body since it is inextricably linked with mind and spirit. At base level, clean nutrition is vital. We cannot sustain basic energy or cognitive functioning if we are overfed and undernourished. A diet high in processed foods tends to offer more calories than anyone needs without providing much in terms of vitamins and minerals.

Physical movement is incredibly important and has been linked to positive health outcomes for people of every age and social group. My own research on depression in military veterans indicates that veterans who report being physically inactive are almost twice as likely to suffer from depression.[3]

The sort of physical movement that appeals to a person will vary widely. I ran marathons and suffered through hip pain and stress fractures afterward, thinking that these were completely acceptable outcomes when exercising. In the military, extreme fitness is popular, and overuse injuries are common. Healthy physical practice pushes boundaries without going to injurious excess and believes in finding challenge through diversity rather than simply doing more of the same. That boundary is different for every individual, and what is a healthy physical practice for one person may not be for another.

It sounds a bit vague because what works for each person will differ. We need to look for those feelings of joyful, spent satisfaction and relaxation to know what counts as self-care for our bodies. To build resilience, healthy practices that lower stress, regulate the nervous system, and bring attention to muscular imbalances are the building blocks of a self-care regimen.

Adaptive wellness opportunities for veterans can provide important education about physical movement meant to strengthen, not tear down or endure. I have done work with adaptive functional fitness, trail running, and yoga. Quite frankly, I find them all appealing! There is no single modality that provides the answer for all veterans, but several have a track record of working well.

The answer for most of us includes a couple of different movement practices that also remind us to fuel our bodies kindly, to spend some time outdoors, and to notice our own *breath in* and *breath out*. It may include a beloved activity done differently, or some untried practice that feels foreign but interesting.

I'm a yoga teacher, and one cannot expect to read a chapter on self-care and not hear my plug for the practice. Yoga works really well for veterans because it can be both wildly challenging and incredibly relaxing. When I teach a room full of skeptical veterans with traditional fitness backgrounds, I am sorry to say that I often try to challenge them a bit because I know the tribe's temperament. If I hurt them, they come back. As they sweat and struggle through a flow sequence, many start to respect the mat a bit more sincerely and feel more open to the other benefits of practice. Yoga can be a tremendous value adder for veterans looking to deescalate their stress response, and is worth mentioning in some detail. It can be incredibly powerful for individuals looking to add to their own self-care practice skillset.

Interestingly, many people still look at this incredibly healing practice with a fearfully skeptical eye. Yoga is not a religion and it is not hard to learn. While you could hurt yourself doing it, that isn't very likely with a savvy teacher. It is also not the sole province of women who can bend like pretzels and fit into color-coordinated spandex.

I promise.

***

As I mentioned previously, I didn't choose to learn about balanced physical training. I was forced to alter the way I thought about physical practice when I caused a serious injury to my back in the weight room. It didn't *happen* to me; I honestly broke my own back by overtraining and lifting while stressed out, tired, and careless.

I showed up at the gym that day both hungry and upset about a dissolving relationship, and I know now that I should do very few things in this world while hungry. I moved really fast between sets so that I could get out of there and eat something. Skipping the workout wasn't an option in my mind, even though it was my second one that day.

I bent down to lift my partner's bar with straight legs and heard something pop as I stood up. I hit my knees as every colorful term I'd ever heard flew out of my mouth. The gym screeched to a silent halt as I swore. Everyone turned to look at me with concern—it sounded like a crazy woman was ranting, I am sure.

Once a friendly nurse got me a hamburger, I had time in the emergency room to do some thinking about how I had been treating my body, and what became clear wasn't pretty. Something had to change if I was going to be able to walk past the age of forty.

As I worked to stay active and avoid impact while recovering, I had to leave behind fitness in my usual driven fashion in favor of a more balanced, wellness-focused movement modality. I couldn't just go run some stairs or hills; I had to get more creative. At the bequest of my physical therapist with the charming Scottish accent, I found myself on a yoga mat. Mostly because of that accent, I would have tried ballet had he asked me to. It seemed the most unlikely of places, but I liked it so much that I spent some time reading about yoga, then I looked into teacher training. I'm a complete nerd, and when something surprises me I head off to Google or the library to figure out why. I was really fascinated to read the plethora of research results that make a strong case for yoga as a self-care modality.

There are many definitions and branded phrases to describe the form of therapeutic yoga used to treat patients. Typically, yoga interventions involve still, seated meditation, physical movements of varying difficulty levels, and instructional seminars on individual peace, spirituality, and stress management.

Yoga links breath to bodily movement in poses meant to create both strength and flexibility. It can be practiced in a variety of styles, but it always involves an element of focused attention on breath and body. In a society where we are often moving too fast, yoga asks us to do more than simply exercise; it asks us to slow down and pay attention, activating our parasympathetic nervous system and giving our tissues and minds space to recharge.

One of the best reasons to give yoga as a fitness modality a try is that the science supports its usefulness. The practice of yoga has been successful in reducing the immediate and chronic effects of stress and enhancing overall health, and it offers physical and emotional benefits that may assist in the prevention and treatment of serious illness. The worth of mindful movement has been tested in cancer patients, the elderly, the depressed, and the hyperactive.

In particular, yoga does great things for mental well-being. A 2007 study published in the *Journal of Cognitive Behavioral Therapy* charted the self-reported quality of life improvements in two groups of physically healthy participants currently participating in Cognitive Behavioral Therapy (CBT) for stress-related anxiety. The intervention group continued the therapy and participated in an intervention based on meditation and physical yoga. The control group continued their regimen of CBT alone. The group incorporating yoga into their routine reported significantly higher quality of life indicators.

Chronic pain has been successfully treated with yoga in several studies. The *Clinical Journal of Pain* follows closely interventions of a complementary and alternative nature and published in 2011 the latest results from a long-term study on military veterans. Veterans with nonmalignant pain undertaking a yoga practice and meditation course reported reduced severity of their pain. Another study in Washington DC in 2014 found that not only could six weeks of yoga reduce patients' pain but it could reduce blood cortisol levels.

Distress compromises the immune system because fight or flight views sending energy to staving off illness as nonessential. Long term, chronic stress causes a host of problems for people trying to stay healthy because their T-cells are underresourced and unable to do their jobs! Immune function in particular has been shown to improve with yoga-based intervention. A study among college-aged females practicing for twelve weeks showed functionality improvements at the middle and study-completion testing points.[4]

Taking care of our physical bodies goes a long way toward readying us to deal with a crisis when it erupts. Managing stress, eating well, and moving are all important. Because our physical bodies are linked to our mental states, taking care of the bodies takes care of the mind. Rates of depression, anxiety, stress, and stress-related health problems all go down when we become active.[5]

***

Theresa's road to recovery was a long one, but it motivated her to share with other veterans the importance of basic physical and mental self-care. She became a CrossFit coach and yogini. She found teachers who taught her to meditate and pray, inviting kindness and calm into her daily thoughts. She went to physical therapy school and earned a clinical doctorate, fascinated with the way the body's movement could bring happiness and healing.

The ugly inner voices quieted.

Today, Theresa is Dr. Larson. She works as a physical therapist and mobility coach who helps people figure out the importance of physical self-care and movement optimization. She sees the difference she makes in every patient, but none more than her Wounded Warriors. Each week she holds a free class for military and veteran athletes suffering from stress injuries, traumatic brain injuries, or who are recovering from surgery or an amputation. The class bills itself as an adaptive strength opportunity, but it does more than teach people who lost a limb how to train in a new way; it creates a community.

They start the session with introductions, sharing embarrassing stories and getting the scoop on who everyone is dating. Whether their injuries are visible or not, they relearn how to love movement and work on making it a daily practice. Through humor, shared physical pain, and a coach who has been through a few of her own hard times, they build a team in that gym.

You got this, buddy.

The space between them lessens over the course of the workout, and their resilience gets stronger as their bodies do.[6]

Chapter 8

WARRIOR FAITH

Be still, and know that I am God.—Psalm 46:10

I don't regret my time in Iraq. I volunteered to go, I loved the people with whom I served, and I was fortunate beyond measure to come home safely. Most days during my deployment, I was convinced of my own invincibility. I was always armed, rarely alone, and at twenty-five that was good enough for me. Whether we were inside or outside the wire, I felt pretty confident that I had control over whether I was alive or dead.

That all changed on a Friday night.

Friday night didn't mean anything different on deployment than other nights of the week, but it was a psychological thing—it still felt like Friday to us. I had a small crew of fellow company grade officers that I could always count on to be excited about the nonevent too. We would occasionally buy a nonalcoholic beer and pretend it was a completely normal week's end. We'd tell a few dumb stories, laugh a bit, and then go back to work.

It was a way to connect with one another and a way to relax like we might at home. That night, we were doing exactly that, sitting on the roof of a concrete building inside the base. The air was balmy, but a breeze was blowing if you climbed high enough. We were probably talking about our significant others back home, and we were feeling pretty darn pleased with ourselves.

One moment we were laughing at the sensitive guy we loved tormenting with our teasing, and the next instant the quiet was shattered.

There was a whine overhead, a whistle that sounded different than the incoming mortar rounds with which I had grown surprisingly comfortable. It was sharper somehow, and I flinched noticeably as a fireball zipped past my field of vision.

The rocket crashed below us into a section of cans that we used as sleeping quarters, sparking like a firework and making a shrill screeching sound as metal tore into aluminum.

We ducked and zipped down the building's wall to take cover, wondering who was in the can that just got hit, hoping it was no one we knew too well.

Glad I was on this roof instead of in there . . .

It was one random rocket—far from spectacular. It made an impressive show of tearing apart the sleeping quarters that it hit, but it hadn't hurt any of us. Turned out, the can housed an acquaintance, another young lieutenant who would be grateful the rest of his life that he'd been on a mission that night.

It really wasn't that big of a deal, which is why I couldn't explain why it sent me into such a funk.

I walked around the next few days feeling down, unable to put my finger on what was bothering me. It wasn't fear, really. It felt colder than that.

I knew to brace myself when we left the Forward Operating Base, but I thought we were pretty safe inside the wire.

That could have gotten any of us.

If it did, what if I had been walking along with no clue? In the shower? Out jogging?

Would that even count as a combat death?

If it happens, is it going to happen in some pointless way?

I finally realized that I'd lost my pretty illusion of control. If I died in Iraq it might be in a completely random way. An incoming rocket might simply choose my building. An IED might just glance my vehicle. There likely wouldn't be the chance for a firefight, to make a difference against a known threat, or to protect the people I cared about. If it came, death would be out of my control, random, and wouldn't fit into some heroic fantasy. It depressed the hell out of me.

If I'm not in control, who is?

The Meaning of Faith

I often hear that it is hard to find atheists in foxholes, and I believe it. When confronted with a crisis, it is normal to think about our notions of the larger world and our connection to something larger. Facing our own mortality at least caused most of us to pause and consider the question.

To spend a bit of time talking about the role of faith in cultivating resilience, though, requires really understanding what I am speaking of. This chapter isn't about dogma, but I am talking very specifically about faith as it is practiced, not merely conceptualized. There are so many ambiguous terms out there that people use to discuss the intensely personal topic, and I want to be explicit that in this chapter I am speaking of *organized religiosity* when I talk about it.

Researchers talk about religious practices as being organized or not, with motivations for practice as coming from internal or external sources. Organizational religiosity simply means that in addition to holding a personal belief system, a person also attends religious services, meets with small groups, or is involved in other community-related activities such as outreach or volunteer efforts. Nonorganized religious practices are individual and are often conflated with the term spirituality. Spiritual practices are often derived from the self-disciplining techniques of religious adherents, though today we often hear them spoken about in a secular sense. Meditation, chanting, and breath work practiced by Christian mystics are discussed in broader, more inclusive contexts today, particularly in spiritual traditions that are focused on internal exploration and self-fulfillment. Sometimes they are talked about in even more secular senses with a focus on performance enhancement.[1]

We often hear, "I'm spiritual but not religious."

There is tremendous personal utility and some health benefit to personal, nonorganized spiritual practices. However, the majority of religion and health science shows maximum benefit for people involved in organized religious communities, which is why I am focusing on the phrase and the practices associated with it in our discussion of how to build resilience.

For me personally, faith means really spending time on the disciplines that bring me closer to God, not for purposes of getting healthier, but for meaning and joy and hope. This means being part of a life-giving church community and spending time in prayer, reading scripture, and talking through it all with people who are similarly engaged and searching.

As mentioned already, it is interesting that when we look at the research on faith, religious affiliation is the sort of variable that yields both practical and statistical significance, meaning it matters in people's lives as well as in some statistical model. Scientists have found two religion variables that yield the most significance, even when other related or modifying variables are present. If someone is involved in organized religious practices (church attendance, small groups, volunteering) and holds those beliefs dearly (subjective religiosity), they are less likely to suffer from a host of health issues.

The bottom line is this: we are wired to connect with God and with each other. Studies overwhelmingly affirm this. Much like exercise, religion offers true protective effects against heart disease, depression, and even cognitive decline. Religiosity is correlated positively with improved mental and physical well-being, and is important for people coping with trauma. How intensely involved a person is in their faith community strengthens the positive impact it can have.

Faith impacts human health psychologically, socially, and physically, because most religious traditions encourage healthier choices and philanthropic acts. I will spend time in this chapter discussing the way religion motivates people to volunteer, which as we noted when discussing social support's role in resilience, has a massively beneficial effect on human health. People who identify as religious have lower rates of mental health problems, particularly depression or depressive symptoms.[2]

Behavioral Benefits of Religious Involvement— Healthy Living and Social Support

Behaviorally, belonging to a religious community promotes healthier lifestyles and offers social support. In a secular social contract, support is both given and offered. People of faith believe that it becomes their duty to offer social support when people are in times of great need, even as illness or personal problems prevent them from giving much back.

This may explain why studies show that social support from religious communities yields greater health benefits than other types.[3]

After the birth of my first baby, the women in my small group from the Church of the Highlands showed up each night with meals. I was new at the motherhood game, fumbling, and desperately trying to keep my wailing son happy by never putting him down. We all might have starved to death had it not been for those women. Shortly after that, we moved away for a new job and left the church community. Everything they did for us was done with no expectation of reciprocity, as they all knew about our pending relocation. These are acts of kindness I will never forget.

I grew up around religion in a bit of a stiff form. I well remember picture books with Bible stories enchanting us kids, but church wasn't a place I saw people light up and come together. It felt like a ritual that we had to do, not something that we enjoyed and felt part of. As kids, we kept it fun for ourselves in totally inappropriate ways. I definitely remember secretively torturing my siblings in the pew next to me when we said prayers that involved holding hands. We would try to prompt one another to make a noise (and get in trouble) by squeezing too hard. I would roll my eyes at my younger sisters wiggling with impatience during long church services, even as I wiggled impatiently next to them.

I grew up to be a bit of a lapsed Christian, but that was because I was really just a lazy believer. I made time for all sorts of things but very rarely the study or practice of faith. As it does when we take our eyes off Him and focus on other things, my closeness to God dwindled to minimal levels during this time; I worked many a Sunday rather than go to church.

When I became a Marine Corps Officer, my faith life took even more of a backseat to everything else I was doing. I believed that I had time for my Marines and our mission, for training my body in intense and sometimes damaging ways, but nothing else.

After that rocket shocked me into thinking about it again, I realized how long it had been since I had even said a prayer.

I think I have forgotten how to talk to God.

My first instinct was to get right on that, attack the problem, and make a plan to figure it out. Maybe I could write the plan in a journal and color code it somehow?

Probably need to snag a few more highlighters . . .

Maybe a few prayers will keep us safe in the middle of this craziness.

I tried in my clumsy way, but planning to pray and trying to figure out how to do it seemed somehow unsatisfying.

I really don't think this is how it is supposed to go.

Something felt off about simply asking God to get involved in keeping me in one piece, especially after not having spoken in years. My focus was still just on everything in front of me.

> The purpose of prayer is not to inform God what needs to be done on earth; the purpose of prayer is to align ourselves with his realities in heaven. Prayer is not about him coming down—he's already here with us through his Spirit. Prayer is about us being lifted up; it's choosing to look up and beyond, choosing to yield to his ways and not begging like a spoiled child for our own desires to be fulfilled . . . be assured, when something is happening to you, God wants to do something in you.[4]

Despite my own shortcomings trying to return to faith, I made it to Kuwait safe and sound, ready to fly back to the States. A month later, as a double-stacked mine ripped through his tactical vehicle and all of our lives, my little brother beat me home on a medevac plane.

I guess God wants to do something in me, because a hell of a lot is happening to me and mine . . .

Pretty words have never been what most compel me, and I got to see my family's faith in action during the time we came together during his recovery. We were there for him and for each other in the ways that really mattered while my brother fought off infections and tried to piece his body back together.

God is everywhere in this hospital.

I watched my father hold an unknown young Marine's hand through narcotic-induced nightmares.

I watched my brother's fiancé work all day and spend every night in a chair by his hospital bed.

I saw the corpsman who had saved my brother's life focus on the people coming to see him rather than his own missing limbs. I won't forget the youth of his young wife next to him, or watching him comfort his mother from his own recovery bed.

I watched the courage with which they all fought for mobility, independence, and a restored sense of self.

I watched as the sweetest nurse, the young one who always answered questions while looking in your eye, teased my brother and made everyone on the ward smile. There was steel in her spine, I could see it.

There was so much to believe in when I looked at these people, and some were only nineteen.

When He has tested me, I shall come forth as gold (Job 23:10, KJV).

It was in a hospital room one night that I felt God talk to me again the way I remembered from younger years. I was tired but trying to stay awake to occasionally press my brother's morphine drip so that he could stay asleep. I hadn't asked anyone if that was a good idea, but I thought I was helping since he hadn't gotten a lot of rest lately.

I hate seeing him in pain.

I was raging inside in a way I could barely understand. I felt guilty that I was walking around without the tiniest scratch and that I'd been cracking jokes and packing bags to leave when he could have used me by his side at Baghdad Surgical. It felt wrong that so many people were suffering like this, that I didn't know how else to help besides sit there. I felt angry and vengeful and hostile toward someone, everyone—anyone really. I wanted to trade places with my little brother.

At least I can help him sleep through some of this pain if I keep clicking this little button.

He woke up with a sharp inhale and looked at me in alarm. He was gasping for breath with a funny sucking sound and terror shot through me.

Kate—something's wrong! My heart is racing!

I ran and got the night nurse, who flew in behind me and pressed some buttons on the ten different machines surrounding him. She explained to me in the kindest way a medical professional ever could that pressing that morphine drip while he slept was not helpful. It didn't keep my brother pain free and sleepy; it risked sending him into respiratory arrest.

She should have slapped me upside the head and told me I could've killed him, but she was gentle about it.

I can be a real idiot sometimes—super confident as I move forward with no idea what I am doing.

After he fell back asleep, I resumed my spot in the chair, utterly deflated. I felt vulnerable and imperfect and scared—all emotions I never usually let myself feel anymore. In the quiet of his dark room I felt my hard façade let down, and I wept quietly as I asked God for help, for peace, and for healing for all the beautiful and shattered people around me. It was time for a personal return to faith.

I can't do everything by myself. I'm not as together or competent as I pretend.

It was a much-needed humbling.

I asked a close friend to pray with me later and to ask Jesus to assume control and presence in my life and heart again. I had no idea how to follow up on it, or what was ahead of me in the years to follow, but it was a start. Though I would fall off my well-intentioned path dramatically in coming years, it was a beginning.

> We were crushed and overwhelmed beyond our ability to endure, and we thought we would never live through it. In fact, we expected to die. But as a result, we stopped relying on ourselves and learned to rely only on God, who raises the dead. And he did rescue us from mortal danger, and he will rescue us again. We have placed our confidence in him and he will continue to rescue us. (2 Corinthians 1: 8–10, NLT)

***

Military personnel are more likely to speak about stressful issues with chaplains than clinicians.[5] As a result, religious leaders have a prominent role to play in helping veterans access help and get plugged back in to their communities. Studies back-up the simple truth that encouraging faith practices also encourages health and happiness. Communities of faith can be profound sources of social support, healing, and hope for veterans returning home and experiencing the stress and possible trauma of transition.

I laughed when a friend told me that for a long time he had trouble personally believing in God, but he and his family continued to go to church. He got the value of the weekly ritual even as he struggled with his own questions about the religion of his youth. He knew that if something happened to him on his next deployment, their church family would reach out to support and love his wife and children.

Take care of widows and orphans, right?

I smiled because I got it: it is easy to know that faith is important and probably a good idea but often hard to carve space in our noisy lives for our own organized religious practice. I knew all about God for years without making time or space for Him to connect in a real way in my own life.

My friend came home from what should be his final deployment about a year ago. There were things he didn't want to talk about, even with those of us who knew him well. What struck me most was his eagerness to get back to church with his family. There was a difference to his Sunday choices and the way he spent time with his kids. He was joyfully alight from the inside, legitimately happy and calmer. My friend had come to God in his own time, in his own private way.

It was a new beginning.

I had lots of new beginnings like that, mostly because although I was often well intentioned, I wasn't always up for the hard part of practicing faith. For many people who grew up in religious communities, which for me was a Catholic church, it can be hard to always feel at home among those who seem to be blissfully certain. My questioning and searching didn't feel truly welcome, I was dismayed at visible hypocrisy or abuse cover-ups, and my politics and priorities didn't always align with the cultural questions being debated. I didn't think I had the time to really connect, get involved, or engage in some grand theological exploration.

I felt a bit too good for it all and walked away from religion with the excuse that I was staying above the fray. It was easier to work from a purely secular standpoint, even though that wasn't an authentic place of wholeness for me. For too many of us, it is easier to disengage when faith gets human and complicated. I just avoided all the divisive theological questions and took the intellectually and spiritually lazy route. I thought I could hang on to my belief in God without actually being a part of a flawed, human institution. I tried to be a Christian on my own, and that never worked out as I hoped.

When I read the work of Sarah Bessey, I felt a click of recognition absorbing her words on becoming a parent. Questions of belief that one fumbles around with carelessly (or even brushes aside in frustration) as an independent individualist matter differently when crafting a home for a baby. My path had several false starts, but for me the difference became motherhood. Bessey writes in her beautiful memoir *Jesus Feminist*, "My mother was drawn to God through my birth . . . her great love for her daughters put her feet on the path toward the empty tomb and the risen Christ and his invitation to recover her true life . . . now I understood."[6]

My son made a practicing believer out of me the second I knew he was on his way. My annoyed, superior, lazy turning away wasn't an option anymore. In parenting, I knew I had hit a wall I wouldn't be able to jump with a simple training program, and I think I for the first time knew I faced a challenge I couldn't meet in my own strength (that favorite lie I always told myself).

I couldn't begin to pretend that I knew everything or held the world up and together on my own brilliance and strength when faced with my baby's presence. I won't be a limiting feature in his life by continuing to believe my own self-delusions of competence and total independence. I'll find other ways to disappoint and embarrass him, I am sure, but not here. It is my job to bring my best forward each day for him, to help him hone his gifts and make a difference in the lives of those around him. Let's be real—I cannot do that sleep-deprived and on my own strength. *I'm just not that good.*

I looked at his roundly serious face right after he was born and was overwhelmed by the light he already had within him. New moms all rave a bit about their babies, but I know it is more than the oxytocin talking. This caterwauling baby brought a quarreling family into the same room, replaced frowns with smiles, and motivated people to set aside judgments and just love one another. He was our unexpected miracle. We named him Matthew after his uncle—my brother and my lifelong friend.

In truth, he is also named for a New Testament verse.

> *In the same way, let your light shine before others, that they may see your good deeds and glorify your Father in heaven (Matthew 5:16, NIV).*

Psychological Benefits of Religious Involvement—Hope and Positivity

It isn't just attendance at religious services that offers healing to people. Belief and connection with God does something unique to us when reinforced through personal practice and supported by a community. Peter Haas is one of my favorite authors, and he talks about two powerful tools that infuse faith practices with true, healing meaning: *constant meditation* and *inconveniently godly friends.* "For every problem we could have, God has a promise to answer it. But knowing God's word isn't enough—believing that it is true is what counts."[7]

Belief is mentally healthy and it is what we are neurologically wired for.

I am a health scientist with no training or skills in theology. Though there are a million reasons to cultivate a relationship with God, I invite you to read the work of savvier pastors to talk about those. In my work on religion and resilience, I focus particularly on those reasons for belief that show up in our bodies. In Psalm 139, David sings about being *fearfully and wonderfully made*, and truer words are hard to find.

Whether speaking from a secular or religious position, the question of divine connection always comes up when one discusses human mental health and happiness. My favorite researcher in the field of social work spent years immersed in her interviews with people about happiness, vulnerability, and shame. Dr. Brown's work surprised her. She found that faith mattered a great deal to really happy people. "Without exception, spirituality—the belief in connection, a power greater than self, and interconnections grounded in love and compassion—emerged as a component of resilience."[8]

Social psychologists discuss human needs as happening in hierarchy, with the need for transcendence being the highest. In this secular sense, transcendence is discussed as the need to help others seek deep meaning and to discover it for oneself.

Always, humans are wired to seek God and connect with one another.

Seeking God alone or in groups often requires focused and attentive prayer. Devotional time of this nature alters the human brain in a manner different than the mindfulness meditation appropriate for stress management, which is discussed in other chapters as a self-care and a mental fitness training method. While meditation activates the parasympathetic nervous system to calm the body's stress response, focused prayer actually calms the threat response while simultaneously stimulating the brain toward feelings of union with others and with a higher power.

Neuroscientist Andrew Newberg at the University of Pennsylvania has worked with respected research teams to show us exactly what happens during attentive prayer of this sort. The posterior parietal lobe that normally orients us in space and time and offers feelings of "self vs. other" deactivates a bit, while the section of the brain that creates feelings of compassion and empathy activates.

These changes, and others improving focus and emotional regulation in the prefrontal cortex, become permanent over time, as the brain acts like a muscle that can be trained. Neurons and synapses get used to connecting during prayer and cause our compassion and sense of loving connection. "Intense long-term contemplation of God . . . appears to permanently change the structure of those parts of the brain that control our moods, give rise to conscious notions of self, and shape our sensory perceptions of the world."[9]

The book of Romans talks about prayer and faith renewing the mind, and brain scans have demonstrated that such renewal is real.

Be transformed by the renewing of your mind (Romans 12:2, NIV).

This renewal leads to action in this world that optimizes health for the faithful and improves the communities in which they live.

Psychologists know that rumination and intense self-focus are unhealthy for mental wellness. Christian scripture encourages philanthropic focus on others' needs, and prayer's impact on the compassion centers of the brain prompts concern and focus beyond one's own walls. Interestingly, studies have shown that religious Americans are more likely to do anything from donate blood to help a sick neighbor dealing with depression. Among older adults, 70 percent of volunteer work happens in a religious setting. Americans who self-report going to church give four times the amount of money to charity that their secular neighbors do, and they are more likely to do volunteer work with the poor, infirm, and elderly twice-over.[10]

I don't share the health and community-building benefits of faith to set Christians apart in any self-aggrandizing way, but rather to demonstrate the importance of spiritual health for any person, and to veterans struggling with reintegration in particular. Medical professionals and clinicians have begun focusing on the importance of spirituality to their patients simply because it is important to so many. Medical schools offer classes on spirituality and healing, and researchers convene at major institutes focusing on the religion and health realm.

The Mysterious Benefits of Religious Involvement—Divine Healing

For believers, the idea that God has the power to make a difference in our daily lives and in our health is easy to wrap our minds around. For the clinical community, this is much more challenging—talking about divine intervention means trying to apply the scientific method to religious mysticism.

Stay with me here, and let's talk about this particular aspect of religion and health with an open mind.

The modern medical and health research communities are in agreement about the behavioral, social, and psychological ways that religion benefits human health. There are simply too many studies and data to refute this. But can we take this conversation a step farther?

An interesting, emerging field in medicine involves a *theosomatic* approach, which simply means that scientists are looking at the ways experiences with the divine impact the physical body. Studies have looked at the impact of bio-energetic healing, altered consciousness states, and prayer for patients by other people.[11]

With the exception of Western medical tradition, healing traditions have always had a focus on energy or spirit. What a Chinese medical practitioner might call *Qi*, a Christian would refer to as the Holy Spirit. Humans are more than a physical body and a logical mind; we are spiritual creatures. Our personal spirituality is interwoven with our physical bodies and our mental and emotional processes. If we want to optimize our wellness, we cannot think of them as separate, or simply ignore one area like I did for so long.

The question for me became whether I was just saying that I understood health from a mind, body, spirit perspective, or actually believed in the concept enough to invest my time.

If I believed that time spent on my spirituality was important to my overall wellness, could I avoid asking myself what spirituality looked like for me? Could I simply continue to overlook my faith?

There is some interesting research out there on the impact of divine consciousness experiences and healing through absent prayer. The most famous study on the topic was published in the *Southern Medical Journal* in 1988. Researchers looked at 393 adults in a random, double-blind study to see if prayer by Christian groups could help improve outcomes for patients in hospital critical care units. The study was well designed, meaning that the praying volunteers, patients, and medical staff had no idea who was in the control and treatment groups. The treatment was simple: a small handful of prayerful volunteers offered daily petitions for one assigned patient until they were released from the unit. They didn't know details about the patient, just a first name and a condition. There was no contact with the patient. When data were collected, the results were unbelievable. The patients who were prayed for had much better results on everything from heart failure to medication needs. The study was controversial and provocative in the medical community, and many dismissed the results.

Like most things spiritual, the answers to theological inquiries aren't conclusively found in scientific journals. Today, most researchers believe that the data on prayer's effectiveness is not conclusive. I don't know that it is even a question research can and should answer. The 1988 intervention is not the only study out there that arrived at the answer that "prayer is helpful." Over 150 experimental trials have been conducted showing that intercessory prayer has been effective in speeding wound healing, improving mental health, and even reducing complications from AIDS. However, there are also studies available that show no effect at all.[12]

While it is interesting to be aware of the conversations happening in the medical community, it seems silly to look to research to know what we are told we must take on faith. The question of God's existence and interest in our wellness cannot be answered by statistics. Belief is too personal for that and we must come to our own conclusions.

***

Trent didn't see the car coming. His hands were full of papers, his cell phone was glued to his ear, and he was in a hurry as he walked into the crosswalk headed toward his office. The impact was sharp, and the last thing he remembered was hearing a loud snap.

When he woke up, Trent was in a hospital emergency room learning that he was beyond lucky. His encounter with a distracted driver and her small sedan would only leave him with some swollen joints and a few broken ribs. His wife picked him up, gave him a pain pill, and put him gently to bed. Ann was worried—the doctors said there wasn't anything they could do for broken ribs but encourage rest and some time off. The first thing she did when he drifted off was call her mother and her small group leader. "Pray for him, please," Ann said. "He is in so much pain and he has a massive project going on at work! I don't know what we will do if he is down for weeks."

Trent slept for almost seventeen hours, largely thanks to those prescription pain pills. When he woke up, he climbed out of bed and walked out to the kitchen to start the coffeemaker, just as he did every morning. He inhaled deeply before noticing that he shouldn't be able to do that.

Ann just smiled, faithfully.

Today my brother is a husband and father, and my son is named after him. He even goes jogging now and again and dances with his beautifully wild children.

I praise God for his recovery and for the life he gets to have.

It almost didn't happen that way.

***

Things are different for me since making space for a belief in Jesus that also includes a set of active practices and communion with people, rather than those parts of faith being something I passively skip over. I still have to wrestle with thorny questions and agree to disagree with many whose views on politics, culture, or theology don't match my own.

That's okay.

What is no longer an option is to throw my faith out with the debate, no matter how many times I get frustrated or see something that looks like the opposite of what Jesus would have us do. I have to engage, care, come together in community with other seekers and explore the importance of my spirituality to my notion of who I am as a person. I'm no longer interested in living a life carved into parts, and I won't offer that old version of me to my family.

She was kind of a jerk.

I'm unabashedly singing and clapping and praising these days. My professional efforts aren't about getting the next pay raise or promotion, and I love, love, love my *inconveniently godly friends*. I don't chafe with angry thoughts and bitterness all the time, and my focus is outward on helping veterans and Wounded Warriors in my community.

It has made all the difference.

God reminds me every day about the beauty present in humanity, and my relationship with Him is no longer rote or incidental. I'm not a naturally generous or thoughtful person, and I need to pay attention to God to keep myself moving in a direction worth heading. Naturally, I am a controlling egomaniac, if I am to be honest with you on these pages! I have to practice my faith in a conscious way and find the "inconveniently godly friends" Peter Haas writes about to help me along a healthy, useful, happy path.

That requires practice, prayer, and most of all people. My faith community today is vitally important for my family.

I worry less about denomination or dogma than about positive examples, truth in deed, joy, and support in a Christian community.

Faith has made me more resilient. It makes me a much better wife and a more patient mother.

If only I had known Him earlier.

Part Three

Making a Difference

Chapter 9

THE WAY FORWARD

B y now, we all agree that there is a problem with the way veterans are transitioning home to civilian life and that this results in some serious public health issues. The question becomes at this point, *how do we make a difference?* Addressing wellness in the military requires a two-pronged approach. First, we need to focus on savvy programs for veterans who have already served, particularly the younger veterans of Iraq and Afghanistan who are more likely to be walking around with symptoms of undiagnosed depression.[1]

Second, we need to develop a prevention focus and do more to make transition smoother for personnel currently on active duty, and for those who will serve in the future. Transition education should be more than a one-week class on the way out of active duty, and a focus on resiliency training in the active component can smooth the rougher spots.[2] If resilience can be cultivated, trained, and taught, we can test for it.

We can craft programming that is developed specifically for female veterans, for veterans going back to school, or for veterans with families. We can deliver such interventions with the benefit of careful, focused program evaluation data behind them—making sure that what we are offering is useful, culturally appropriate, specialized, and evidence based. At present, much of the well-intentioned programming being offered lacks real evaluation metrics.

The starting points are out there and evident most clearly in the nimble nonprofit community. Well-intentioned volunteers have worked tirelessly to create opportunities for healing that involve learning a new skill, making a new friend, or finding new purpose. I have been excited to work on such programs in the corporate and nonprofit sectors, and today partner with another Marine veteran to deliver our version of resilience-building seminars. We're constantly tweaking the curriculum as we evaluate with increasing rigor, but the stuff that works is always the same. Social support, self-care, and spirituality make any of us healthier, and select techniques in each area can help improve quality of life.[3]

Veterans Leading Veterans

When working with both active duty and veterans, peer leadership is incredibly useful. Warrior subculture creates a powerful mandate for peer-to-peer outreach. Any message aimed at promoting wellness must come from members of the community in order to be deemed credible. Recall that a major sentiment expressed by separating service members is a feeling of disconnect from civilians, especially after a combat deployment.

In the military community, the best program implementation cases are found within participatory research frameworks. Because warrior cultures have their own temperaments, they are typically exclusive and mistrustful of outsiders with different life experiences.[4]

Programs have a chance to work best when veterans or active duty personnel have a hand in planning and implementing them. The 2010 case study highlighted in chapter 4 is a terrific example, sharing one Michigan pilot program's experience with "buddy-to-buddy" peer support programs. What made the program uniquely successful wasn't the content; it was the delivery channel chosen. The team of Michigan researchers keenly understood the need for audience-centered communication and partnered with unit leadership to institute a program that was completely peer led. This decision came out of the qualitative research they conducted in the unit prior to thinking about a program. Interviewees said things like, "If you haven't been there, you don't get it" and "Other veterans can be trusted." The research team considered concepts of warrior culture and sought to design a program that spoke the correct language, using an understanding of social norms to change the culture of treatment avoidance.

Another reason the success of the program is so noteworthy is that it worked with reserve personnel after deployment. National Guard soldiers, like all reservists, often face stresses additional to those faced by active duty troops. Reservists don't come from as insular of a military community and may lack support services in civilian community settings. Particularly because PTS symptoms are very likely to be misread as behavioral deviance, stigma may be even more difficult to overcome in community settings removed from the active duty military component.

Programming in Communities

There have been exciting successes as motivated nonprofits, academic research teams, and service providers of every stripe have made efforts to help veterans navigate their life post-service and post-war.

Too many organizations to name have established nonprofits and worked to provide therapeutic services for military veterans. From animal therapy opportunities to outward bound adventures, kind-hearted servant leaders have stepped forward to create programs and bridge gaps. These groups offer a hand, a new experience, and attempt to save and improve lives. The Wounded Warrior Project funds many of these as partner nonprofits, and has been instrumental in getting resources out to lesser-known groups.

In particular, organizations created by and geared particularly toward younger veterans of the Iraq and Afghanistan conflict era have brought important opportunities at the community level. They all focus uniquely on empowerment narratives, asking veterans to get engaged as they participate in services and programs, encouraging them to give back, get off the sofa, and plug in to their local community. The Mission Continues, Team Rubicon, and TeamRWB are prime examples of groups that work to give veterans a new social community centered around a common purpose. Whether that purpose is community service, disaster relief, or physical fitness, the intent is the same and the program evaluation success rates are noteworthy.

Roger was the first in his family to walk into a recruiter's office, and when he came home to share the news that he had just enlisted in the National Guard, he had to explain *why* to a set of very concerned parents. He had a plan though. He was going to serve six years, get help with college tuition, and get out of his small town in Alabama to do something professional for a living. He wanted to travel beyond the borders of the rural fields he had seen his whole life and talk to people other than those with whom he had grown up.

Roger knew Guard service might mean a call-up; he'd read that part of the enlistment contract. Still, he really didn't expect the call he got one afternoon. No way around it even if he had wanted one. His sergeant first class was clear on the phone: he needed to pack his bags and get down to the unit within forty-eight hours. They were headed to the sandbox.

Roger flew over on a civilian airplane, which seemed weird to him after seeing nothing but gray military aircraft for so long. There was actually a flight attendant there to offer him a beverage. It made the landing in Kuwait feel surreal. Bored and hot, Roger and the guys in his Company kicked around a couple of days waiting for their flight across the border.

The next transport in on a military aircraft was a little less fancy, and when the descent was sharp and nauseating, Roger knew they had just made a combat landing.

It started to feel a little more real then.

They turned over with the unit they were there to relieve—a group of active-duty soldiers who had been running convoys all over northern Iraq the last twelve months. The relief-in-place was shortened to "RIP," and it was fast and furious. Roger went out on a couple of convoys with the guys who had been doing it, listened more than he talked, and then the AO[5] was theirs.

Roger spent a lot of time waiting on the hood of his HMMWV for convoys to kick off. He got really, really good at sleeping in spurts on that vehicle or beside it in the staging area. They'd roll out each evening on patrol, clearing routes for the massive trucks that were hauling supplies all over the country.

Driving was uneventful much of the time. His job was to be fast, know the unit's reaction plan, and keep his guys safe when stuff started going boom.

He thought it would happen more often. They found several odd piles of debris that EOD had to come up and detonate. Sometimes the pile was a bomb and the controlled detonation looked like fireworks to the guys paused along the MSR. Sometimes it had just looked like a bomb to a sharp-eyed gunner, and they were on their way faster sans the dramatic light show when EOD cleared it.

It became routine for Roger to drive erratically and scan the sides of the road for wires, to drive fast and keep a perfect distance from the vehicle in front of him. Roger's eyes stayed sharp, and he got used to driving without headlights in pitch black. He felt good about his chances and their skill. Leaving the wire stopped freaking him out every time. The days and nights started to blend.

They were conducting their own RIP with replacement guys when it happened. They were almost headed home, and he was pretty psyched about seeing the stewardess with the beverage tray again.

It must have been remote detonated, they'd all say later, *and the bomb maker sucked at his work.*

There was no sign of the device on the road down which they had just been speeding. The IED came mysterious and fast as it blew the HMMWV's left tire, lifting vehicle into the air a couple of feet. It crashed back down onto the roadway with a screech, and the three of them braced for what they expected to come next. They waited.

No secondary.

No rounds coming in.

No tracers flashing by.

It was a quick stop, a fast repair, and they were back on their way, but something shifted for Roger. He couldn't stop hearing the crack and feeling that little lift. Couldn't stop thinking that he was trapped.

He stopped sleeping.

When he got home, he had no idea who to talk to. He knew guys who had been through way worse things than him—he was lucky. There was no way he could complain about anything when all of them walked away from Iraq in one piece.

People kept asking him questions that seemed ridiculous, and he decided to leave his little town to go to college, even though there was a perfectly good tech school down the road. Not necessarily to avoid the questions, but just to start over. He got his GI Bill set up at a community college a few hours away and moved into a little apartment.

He still wasn't sleeping.

Roger went to orientation and sat next to a pretty redhead who kept playing with her iPhone. It went off suddenly, and she groaned.

Ugh. My mom is tracking me again.

The phone rang, and the redhead began chatting with her worried mom.

I'm at school, Mom; we're about to start this welcome seminar!

Roger stood up and moved a few seats away. He felt ancient and wondered if he belonged here with these college kids whose parents were keeping tabs on their cell phones. It felt like another world.

Programming for Student Veterans

After WWII, 2 million veterans used their funding from the GI Bill to go to college. Today, college veterans struggle to stay in school; dropout rates are above 80 percent nationally. Some schools are doing better than others, and the University of Arizona is one of them. Recognizing that alienation was a major problem for their campus veterans, Arizona faculty members ran an experiment in their chemistry classes, creating a section made up of just veterans. The experiment started after a chemistry professor became interested in the commonness of stress injury among the military veterans seated in his large, introductory seminars. They had trouble concentrating and contributing, it seemed to him. He tried something unique, creating a veterans-only lab section. This small group became extremely close, and he saw their performance on tests go up.

Bridging the transitory gap for college students who leave the wartime military and enter a civilian college environment where they comprise a tiny percentage of the student body can be extremely helpful. The aim is to keep veterans from hitting a lonely wall of frustration that leads to departure from student life. Universities can also be part of the solution in terms of teaching resilience and self-care, and GI Bill tuition dollars provide financial incentive to do so.

A religious studies professor at Manhattan College in New York named Stephen Kaplan got involved after some of his student veterans approached him to explain how useful they found his coursework on yoga and meditation. The students were in his required Introduction to Religious Studies course and expressed interest in learning more about the yoga and stress management covered in the introductory course. Professor Kaplan saw an opportunity to reach out, and he opened two sections of his Nature and Experience of Religion class specifically for veterans. These sections included an extra focus on relaxation techniques, including a travel component. This component was a retreat of sorts, and students would hop on a plane to leave daily life behind them while they studied different mediation, yoga, and stress management methods in a serene setting.

He wanted to maintain the trip as a central component of the new class but worried that as nontraditional students relying on the GI Bill to fund their educations, his veterans might struggle to come up with the extra funding required to take the class and travel for the experiential portion. When Dr. Kaplan approached Manhattan College's administration, the school stepped forward and funded the travel for his small section of veteran students. As part of his seminar, students would travel to a retreat site in the Bahamas to learn trauma-sensitive yoga and meditation from a woman named Robin Carnes.

Robin has been on the forefront of the mindfulness movement for military veterans for over a decade. She was the first instructor for the trauma-sensitive meditation program at Walter Reed, and her work has been widely featured in the yoga service community. Dr. Kaplan could not have found a more capable instructor for his veteran students. The 2015 program was wildly popular, and through his efforts, the lives of a handful of military veterans struggling to earn a degree, transition to civilian life, and heal from stress injuries were made undoubtedly better. In this class they got a chance to connect with one another, learn some new self-care techniques, and explore their spirituality. Dr. Kaplan is humble about his creative outreach program when asked. "Manhattan College is uniquely positioned to serve its veteran population," Kaplan says. "All MC students are required to take RELS 110, and this course can serve as the intellectual and cultural platform to understand how different forms of yoga, meditation, and stress reduction, found in the religious traditions of the world, help individuals focus their mind and relax." One interested faculty member at a small liberal arts college created a model for student veteran resilience programming. The only thing left to do is formally evaluate it. According to Troy Cogburn, who works as the Coordinator of the veterans' student organization at Manhattan College, "Professor Kaplan and the Religious Studies department are visionaries who have implemented a first-year experience that will positively affect the lives of our veteran student population for years to come."[6]

A Prevention Focus—Training the Active Duty Component

Veterans who have also acquired skillsets in the civilian world lend a trusted hand to the process of improving mental health and transition preparation for military personnel before they leave active service. It is incredibly important that in addition to helping veterans currently struggling, we work to prevent those struggles for current service members. Honing in on the need for culturally sensitive resilience training is one former Army Officer, Dr. Elizabeth Stanley of the Mind Fitness Training Institute.

Dr. Stanley is a former Army captain with deployment experience in Korea and Bosnia. She is a professor of security studies at Georgetown who has invested a great deal of personal time and training energy into behavioral health practices aimed at improving working memory capacity. Dr. Stanley developed the Mind Fitness Training Institute specifically with high-stress organizations like the military in mind, citing the tremendous need to build resilience in a community under repeated and extreme chronic stress (as the norm rather than the exception). The institute's focus is on training instructors and providing services to both veterans and active-duty units, but it also gets involved in research initiatives.[7]

Dr. Stanley partnered with researchers from all over the country to look at stress management in the military with an eye toward turning management of reactivity into a performance enhancer for the active-duty component. Their argument is a sound one. Interestingly, high stress reactivity, naturally occurring adaptation though it may be, hinders the ability of service members to perform complex missions and interact with foreign nationals. The modern battlefield involves interaction with civilians and allies as a matter of course.

Becoming overly reactive as a response to environment hinders that mission. For example, research has shown that soldiers who screened positively for mental health problems were three times more likely to report having engaged in unethical behavior while deployed. Behaviors ran the gamut from unnecessary property damage to noncombatant injury or harm, all diametrically opposed to the United States' mission of winning hearts and minds. These issues leave behind moral injuries with which service members may struggle well into their futures.[8]

Other academic researchers have followed the path of the Mind Fitness Training Institute team and spent time attempting to validate specific interventions for the military community that both formally and informally rely on constructs of Resiliency Theory. A 2011 RAND analysis commissioned by the Office of the Secretary of Defense conducted a systematic evaluation of existing programs in different branches of service. They began by reviewing literature on psychological resilience to identify key content for recommended programming. Interviews with current resilience program leaders identified the presence or absence of such content and inquired about evaluation protocol. Some of the programs were using savvy curriculum, but most lacked good evaluation plans.[9] As a result, study results in environments are rare, though early indicators are promising.

Case studies at the unit level like the "Buddy One" program in Michigan and pilot studies by Dr. Stanley's team have shown promising results, even in the confused climate that characterizes current understandings of depression in today's veterans. These studies all point to the fact that research and program efforts in the training environment for both veterans and active duty must be participatory and peer led whenever possible.

Designing Programs with Solid Foundations

Rigorous evaluation of existing outreach efforts provides the foundation upon which savvy programmers must build. Our best chance for making a difference in the training environment before a service member faces transition stress involves designing programs from a baseline of proven success. The programs should be tailored for audience appropriateness. Cultural competency means not only trying to understand the veteran experience but learning the most effective ways to communicate with different subsets of the veteran and military populations.

Health promotion professionals working to prevent and treat mental health problems like depression and stress illness must understand the confluence of warrior culture and mental health issues in the veteran community. There is ample evidence to support the development of a culturally informed resilience training protocol. Such protocol involves teaching self-care, building social support, and introducing the importance of spiritual and contemplative practices. Evaluating specific techniques under these umbrella constructs is going to be vital in upcoming outreach efforts.

It is important to create programs aimed at post-service quality of life improvement and healing, but the biggest impacts can be made from a prevention angle. The reason for this is that stigma isn't going away, and we can reach more personnel while they are still serving than after they leave. Implementing in participatory fashion in the training environment, rather than in treatment settings, works ideally for veterans who often reject patient identities. That approach works around a major barrier to care for mental health in this population. To combat suicide rates and promote military and veteran mental health, a new approach is required, one that embraces peer education and speaks to the participatory, hard-working ethos of military culture. Resiliency Theory-based programming has potential to meet these needs and may provide a blueprint for success in working with this population.

Focusing on self-care, social support, and faith practices can make anyone more resilient, and it is particularly useful to the military. Resilience creates better performance while serving, and makes transition stress easier to navigate afterward.

Creating a climate of peer-led training at both the unit and individual levels will reduce overall stigma against self-care practices because everyone participates, the program is led by trusted informants, and no one has to take on a patient role to participate. To train is to actively participate, and this is a wellness concept with which service members are already familiar. Framing mindfulness training as a way to "bulletproof your brain" renders palatable a training opportunity designed to create more effective warriors with mental endurance; framing this as promotion of combat fitness, resilience, and mental endurance renders it accessible to the military population.

We have to speak the language of warriors when we talk about resiliency cultivation. By establishing mental fitness as another component of optimal combat readiness, we establish resiliency training as a crucial component of mission preparedness and remove the stigma of such practices for post-deployment troops who may be struggling with stress illnesses of varying degrees. The message can become directive; just as Marines and soldiers learn mission-essential skills and train their bodies for arduous combat, we must adopt practices designed to train and promote health in the mind, body, and spirit in a holistic sense.

Testing Resiliency

When we consider how we could apply these basic recommendations to military veterans seeking relief from reintegration stress or to active duty military preparing for it, we must consider how to make stress management a testable metric. Biofeedback tools exist that can do this, and my future work will involve standardizing a theoretically based, validated training curriculum and using an individual's ability to deescalate their nervous system response as a performance metric. We can use biofeedback testing to make resilience a performance metric for the active-duty component. It turns self-awareness and resilience into standards, and motivates learning, training, practice, and performance in our community's culture.

Checking for DHEA and blood cortisol ratios or conducting periodic blood cortisol checks can be as important as other physical standards are in the military. Biomarkers tell us quickly whether someone is taking time to practice balanced wellness. The future is exciting from both a clinical, training, and prevention perspective. It offers tremendous promise for future military personnel, who will be asked to embrace a holistic wellness training regimen to make them better at their jobs and more resilient in their lives, both during and after their service to our country.

What a difference such self-regulation techniques could have made for me before I navigated that liminal space into a new, civilian identity. What a difference it may make for others.

We can do this—resilience can be cultivated.

Chapter 10

RESILIENT LEADERSHIP

I joke with people that when I drive onto a Marine Corps base and see dated architecture with lots of asbestos insulation, I feel myself exhale contentedly. Really bad haircuts that are undeniably too short look stylish and hip to me. I don't do it anymore, but when I was a new officer I wore my dog tags everywhere, even out with friends in a girly blouse. In my mind, dog tags were the coolest. I, however, was not.

Ahhh, home.

This final chapter is really a letter to my peers. If you made it through all my stories, research overviews, and statistics to reach this point, you must be genuinely interested in how we can serve one another as a community.

I'm not surprised.

I find that it isn't hard for us to want to reach out a hand to one another. We got used to the concept of working as a team and not leaving one another behind at entry-level training. We watched the people who didn't grasp that concept wash out.

We are not yet done with that mission and our sacred duty to one another.

We know how to take care of one another, or at least we think we do. What I would like to suggest in these final few pages is that we may not be doing service to self and one another in all the right ways. We're perpetuating stigma, promoting unhealthy behaviors, refusing to embrace and connect with our civilian communities, and adhering to that tougher-than-thou, silent-suffering code that is killing too many of us.

When I was on active duty, I thought taking my buddy out to the bars was a helpful thing when he shared that he was incredibly depressed over getting dumped. It seemed to me that I had a lot of buddies getting dumped. It is possible that my friends were all subpar significant others, or simply the case that as soon as workups began and deployments loomed, relationships started becoming too much work for both parties. I knew the drill by this time and had favorite bars and wingman jargon at the ready. I had glossy phrases encouraging them to *suck it up* and *get over it* on the tip of my tongue.

I was a horrible friend!

Hindsight has been a bit painful for me the last few years—I made a lot of mistakes because I so firmly believed in the lessons warrior culture taught me. I know now that I could have gone lots of healthier directions to really help that unwillingly single friend. I thought telling people to push through was always the way to go. I thought drinking and partying were useful bandages. Now I know I was participating in creating a culture where people hurting don't feel like they can ask for help.

A few years ago, I had to call a dear friend and former Basic School roommate to apologize for something she barely remembered. It happened when we were stationed together at Parris Island and were truly excited about working as series commanders at 4th Battalion. Our goals were simple: we wanted to set a stellar example for new recruits, help them become Marines, and make sure our drill instructors slept at least an hour or two each week.

We were randomly assigned to our companies, and I was fortunate to walk into a functional and hard-working team environment. She was less fortunate and walked into a true leadership challenge where some unbalanced and strong personalities were creating a great deal of friction for the entire series. She fought tooth and nail to get the team on her page, but it wasn't a fun process. Depressed and wondering if she was doing the right things, she told me she was feeling really down about things and was considering seeking the counsel of a mentor.

I very clearly recall my reaction to her desire to speak with someone outside our chain of command about the admittedly dysfunctional environment she was dealing with. I told her she was whining and malingering, and I encouraged her to buckle down and get the mission accomplished.

Dead serious.

I contributed to the stress and negativity she was dealing with by employing that suck-it-up narrative when she least needed to hear it. I made seeking help and emotional support during a rough professional patch seem like a weak or disloyal thing. I contributed actively to the stigma I rail against in chapter 4 of this book.

My bad.

Didn't I tell you I learn best from failure?

We have a role to play in getting way more real with one another than we typically do. If something is off, we can know what to look for and can seek the outstanding clinical service help that is available to us. We can call stigma against care-seeking what it is: delusional, limiting, and ineffective.

Authenticity is strength and honest leaders are true leaders.

We can lift one another up rather than bemoan stress injury or depression as weakness. They are normal, adaptive reactions to abnormal levels of stress. They are temporary. They can be fixed if we will put in the work and engage in brutal honesty with ourselves and with one another.

And when have we ever run from a challenge?

Set a bar for us—we will clear it.

We can be direct and helpful with ourselves and one another when we see the signs of being out of balance, and we can support one another in healthy ways. Let's be those healthy, supportive, and *inconveniently godly friends* for one another rather than support one another's worst habits and behaviors. Some of my bigger regrets involve those times I needed to be a better version of myself for someone who needed me. I've let people down by not being very self-aware.

Admitting we're wrong about things isn't something we seek out often, I know. What can be hard is accepting that we need to let go of some misplaced pride to find new roles, new civilian identities, new relationships, and new appreciation for the incredible service contributions made in the American civilian community every day. Civilians aren't lazy, apathetic, noncontributors, unless you're simply hanging out with the wrong ones. Find some who are doing tremendous service work—we all need a like-minded tribe.

The veteran blogger who writes *Finding Valhalla* wrote a really frank essay that I have to admit applied to me at one point in my life. I held very tightly to my notions of separation and superiority, and it was one of the least-healthy and most unbalanced things I ever did to myself. It was also wildly disingenuous. There is more than one way to be of service in the world. *Finding Valhalla* coined a comical diagnostic term for egomaniacal veterans who find it tough to connect with civilian peers: "Irritable Veteran Syndrome."

> My worst fear is that we alienate ourselves from the people we fought for by continuing to beat them over the head with the fact we did. I know if I am sick and tired of seeing all the complaining and anger, the average Joe is too. Then the message which I am sure is born out of good intentions gets ignored, and it becomes us against them. The people who we fought for become the people we fight. What a sad day that would be. So be proud. Honor the fallen. Be an example because at the end of the day, if we are as good as we say we are? We won't have to say a damn word. It will show. Who knows, we might actually make a real difference INSIDE the country we fought for.[1]

I love the Marine Corps and our military and have no interest in changing its standards or asking the mission to become kinder and gentler. What *can* change is the way that we approach taking care of ourselves and one another. We can get more efficient and effective, we can make resilience a training standard, and we can create a bar to meet that will really benefit us in the long run.

Let's Be Resilient Leaders, Inside the Military and Out

Dr. Kelly McGonigal of Stanford is one of my favorite academics to read these days. She spends her time putting numbers behind something we know at heart to be true—strength and resilience are mind-sets. We can choose to see stress positively, to let it push us toward performance, or we can adopt a self-defeating mind-set that has a deleterious impact on our physiology.[2]

Psychologists at Stanford's Center for Social and Psychological Answers to Real-World Questions have found that short interventions can improve outcomes for people in almost every area of their lives. These interventions specifically focus on changing one limiting belief. A limiting belief becomes a paradigm through which a person interprets every circumstance or interaction. Setbacks or misunderstandings all become evidence of the limiting belief's truth, and it becomes a vicious cycle of self-limitation.

I didn't get that job because that guy didn't understand what I used to do.
I don't feel comfortable in this group because I am different.

Lead researcher Dr. Walton has had impressive results with interventions addressing the limiting belief that "I don't belong" with marginalized, minority students in Ivy League schools. His intervention worked to shift this belief only slightly, highlighting that feelings of not belonging were a totally normal, commonly experienced part of the freshman college experience that would pass. Over time, he tracked the grades and graduation rates of people who participated in this intervention and in a control group. Amazingly, the students who heard that a bit of loneliness while adjusting was totally normal had better physical health, grades, and self-reported feelings of happiness. Their mind-set as freshmen impacted everything important about their college experience, right down to the cellular level!

If my mind-set can change what is happening chemically in my body, I had better be intentional about choosing my mind-set, right?

Again, let me insert my caveat here. Stress injury is real. When our body's stress response fires at the fight-or-flight intensity level for too long, our nervous systems are going to need help and professional treatment to get back into a regulated state. When we see signs of hypervigilance and reactivity in ourselves or one another, we need to encourage professional assistance and also emphasize that stress injury is a recoverable wound, not a permanent disorder.

Trauma, combat, and unchecked chronic stress can create this injury. We need to know the signs and be supportive about seeking helpful services. We need to avoid telling one another to *suck it up*. Just like running another race on a stress fracture is a dumb idea, telling ourselves to push through a stress injury or a case of depression only makes things worse. Help is there for a reason—to get us back into our desired peak-performing state as soon as possible.

However, the stress veterans face while transitioning to the civilian world does not have to reach traumatic levels and become injurious. Psychologists have done some really exciting studies on mindset interventions meant to help people insert larger context and meaning into their stressors and situate them against a larger mission or set of goals. What they find is that by reminding people of the *why* behind their struggle, they can actually alter the stress hormones released to help create a challenge response or a tend-and-befriend response. These are very different than the intense reactions that can cause injury and are reviewed in detail in chapter 3. These useful forms of performance-enhancing stress make us resilient, effective, and able to handle the mountain in front of us.

We have to help ourselves before we can help others, or we are simply sharing our own imbalances with one another. If peer leadership is going to be useful, we need to have it together for one another! If I could go back in time and undo some of the damage I know I did to peers in the name of being "helpful," I would do so in a heartbeat.

Our Battle for Balance

I hope this book has encouraged you to get authentic with yourself and assess where things stand with your own mental attitude. Would you say you are winning your battle for balance?

Do you have a healthy tribe around you? Social support matters to everyone, and if you don't have positive people in your world, you may need to make some really tough changes. I had to go through an embarrassing and heart-wrenching divorce and get involved in volunteer work to find healthy and sharp people who could help keep me on a healthy path. I also had to get over my own attitudes about the divide between military and civilian folks. It helped that I was going to church and volunteering; I was confronted daily with examples of servant leadership that made it impossible to pretend the only people worth knowing were other service members. That might have been harder were I spending time with people who didn't value similar things. I still love hanging with veterans—I like our particular brand of crazy—but I can learn from, love, and enjoy people from different walks of life now.

Let's get over ourselves, shall we?

Are you practicing self-care? If you are feeding your poor body soda and fast food, exercising in self-abusive ways, or spending way too much time on the couch, consider that answer to be a clear no. *Not okay.* I learned this the hard way when I broke my own back. Humbling and embarrassing as that was, it revolutionized my wellness attitude. I had to learn a few new skills and completely change my attitude toward training. When I am being careful with my body, everything feels easier.

Where do you stand on issues of faith? Whatever you believe, can you honestly say that you have put time and effort into crafting your standpoint? I didn't like some of the hypocrisy I saw in the church of my youth, so my answer was to adopt an intellectually lazy attitude of superiority about Christianity. This wasn't authentic for me, or healthy. There are real, positive, life-giving faith communities out there and people willing to support your experience without getting all annoying and dogmatic on you. Look into it. Invest in your spiritual side in the way that feels honest to you.

***

I hope this book has felt like an invitation. We have so much to contribute outside of the military and away from a combat zone.

Let's do this.

If we are ourselves resilient, we can help others become so.

AFTERWORD

I have always had a special place in my heart for warriors. Some things in life hold such great value they are worth dying for. Warriors embrace such thinking, and they are willing to pay that ultimate price to defend our common values. When others run away from trouble and conflict, warriors run toward these critical incidents and into harm's way. Warriors represent the essence of what we value and respect in servanthood.

A few people are blessed early on in life with an inherent love and desire for their occupational field. That was certainly true for me. I had a burning passion to be a warrior. When I was about four years old, my mother took me with her to pay for a speeding ticket at a Chicago courthouse. She was very good natured about the whole thing as she joked with me, suggesting that she would tell Dad the check she wrote to pay for the fine was for a *pullover*, knowing my father would probably assume she had purchased a sweater. When we entered the courthouse, I saw a deputy sheriff in uniform decked out with his duty equipment, gun belt, crisp, starched uniform shirt and pants, and polished shoes. My heart instantly thumped and skipped a beat, my testosterone surged, and I inherently knew that I wanted to do whatever it was this guy did in life. I had no real idea what that would mean, but I was ready to commit to being a warrior right then and there. "Sign me up," the little boy inside of me cried. I intuitively knew that what this deputy did could be dangerous, but that was part of the rush I felt, and the occupational lure.

By the precocious age of ten, I wanted to be a soldier. I had a heart-felt love and respect for warriors. I wanted to serve. I joined the Army at age twenty, serving in the First Infantry Division (FWD) "Big Red One." I learned a great deal about the meaning of *freedom*, *duty*, and *service* when my military unit visited the Iron Curtain in East Berlin, and

I saw barbed wire barriers and machine guns pointed toward the interior of this country, aimed at those who might attempt escape. After military service I became a California peace officer for the next twenty-eight years, holding positions of patrol officer, field training officer, detective, hostage negotiator, and acting field supervisor.

After retiring from law enforcement, I have pursued writing, consulting, and public speaking that deals thematically with warrior culture-related topics, stress management, and spirituality. Spirituality has played an important role in my life, and it offers great value and benefits for warriors. Scientific research has demonstrated spirituality offers warriors an added dimension of resilience as well as other pragmatic benefits. My own personal spiritual journey is outlined in my book *Turning Adversity Into Success*. Other warrior culture and subculture issues I have studied, researched, and published are in the FBI Law Enforcement Bulletin and in the *Journal of Religion and Health*, in a paper entitled "Warrior Culture, Spirituality, and Prayer." As a guest speaker at Stanford University, I spoke to the institution's staff psychologists, addressing warrior culture and subculture issues.

When we think of *warriors*, occupational groups like police officers and soldiers readily come to mind, but people who demonstrate warrior-like behavior and service to help others in crisis are found in other occupational groups as well. The common precursor we find in warriors is an inner dispositional inclination and commitment to serve and help others that goes beyond just signing up for service. The research data, truth, and lessons in this book are applicable to anyone who appropriates its knowledge and principles. While everyone does not possess the field training skill sets of warriors, everyone has something of value to offer when tragedy strikes. People play different logistical supporting roles in crisis, but often they become united in spirit and in common cause. It becomes a team effort. In studying critical incidents, we find a rich history we can embrace that reveals we all have innate potential and capacity to serve others in various contributing ways. Ordinary people are capable of doing extraordinary things, and in such instances, many become momentary warriors, or they demonstrate warrior-like typology behaviors.

There are spontaneous heroes who unexpectedly encounter a crisis that threatens other human beings in some life-threatening, catastrophic way. The passengers of Flight 93 who fought to overcome 9/11 terrorists on board their aircraft are a perfect example of ordinary American people becoming extraordinary warrior citizens. Such people lived routine, normal lives. They were accountants, students, businessmen and women, traveling salesmen, and homemakers. In a singular moment of human need, they chose to become warriors for the betterment of humankind. The *spontaneous warrior* is not a career warrior by choice or profession. He or she may have such an encounter with destiny only once or maybe twice in their lifetime. In the blink of an eye, the *spontaneous warrior* chooses to give their all to save others, or perhaps just one. Warriors represent the best in all of us.

Warriors are special people who help others who are in need. The needs of the many are great. Warriors give of themselves and put themselves in harm's way because they value the sanctity of life, and they are willing to serve and protect and pay the price of serving. Such altruism represents the ultimate, sacrificial gift of goodness that humanity has to offer.

Warriors are servants, patriots, and check-writers. The term *check-writer* is an idiom. The phrase refers to those who metaphorically sign a blank check, for any amount, up to and including their lives, to serve and protect others, and defend the values we hold dear. The check is paid in full upon demand, at any time of the day or night. Warriors embrace servanthood to protect and serve their country, and their fellow citizens, and to preserve our way of life and our future. Warriors understand freedom is not free.

The cost of military warrior service is profound and beyond what most of us fathom. The price and cost of freedom is most visible with its toll upon warriors. When we see our men and women returning from overseas deployment we see that many are deeply wounded and scarred. Many have sustained serious debilitating amputations and Traumatic Brain Injuries (TBI), but some severe injuries are not visible; they are emotional and mental. The gruesome death, mayhem, and inhumanity they have witnessed is emotionally searing on the human psyche, and such repeated occupational exposures to field conditions are directly and symptomatically linked to PTSD, depression, suicidal ideations, and maladaptive behaviors, making reintegration into civilian life very difficult. Many of these Wounded Warriors are coping on their own, feeling all alone in their grieving process and need for healing.

Many of our military veterans have trouble getting medical treatment and benefits for documented, service-connected injuries such as PTSD, suicidal ideations, depression, and addictions that came about from attempts to numb the emotional pain of their psyche. These heroes withdraw socially from family, friends, and significant others. Wounded Warriors tend to develop a subculture that promotes and embraces maladaptive behaviors because they are trying to cope and survive on their own, and they don't know how to accept help very well when it comes to emotional and mental health matters.

Research studies by the American Psychiatric Association reveal that the majority of military veterans suffering from serious mental health disorders are disinclined to seek professional mental health treatment. These veterans fought as warriors for us, but they don't know how to effectively fight for themselves. Many become homeless and fall through the cracks of our social goodwill and oversight. The suicide rates of our military veterans are currently higher than all other wars we have fought. The loss is profound, horrific, and overwhelming to the extended families, and our government's ability to offer prophylactic intervention with efficacious counseling is limited in scope by bureaucratic poor management.

What we can we do to help returning warriors who come home?

Professional practitioners and therapists need to provide wellness intervention that combats hopelessness and promotes cognitive, critical thinking solution-based options that break subculture barriers and make it permissible for warriors to seek help. Broken hearts and seared psyches need healing. This book will immensely help practitioners better understand the warrior impediments to healing. Warriors need to be trained to disassociate the pursuit of treatment with *weakness* and embrace the reality that it is possible to experience healing and regain a normal healthy life that brings existential meaning, purpose, and wellness.

Many Wounded Warriors need and require professional counseling and other medical services. Those of us who lack professional training should stay within the boundaries of our own limitations and be mindful of the fact that it is not our job to fix people, or treat them for their PTSD symptoms when we have no medical training. Good intentions coupled with ignorance can be harmful, but we can practice our faith and humanity to help promote healing by simply loving Wounded Warriors and standing beside them in practical ways. Good judgment should never preclude us from encouraging people and reaching out to those who are wounded with a kind word or perhaps a job offer.

Healing comes in different forms, but it first begins with hope. The greatest gift we can offer someone is simply acceptance, attention, and love. Such nurturing promotes healing, which is often spiritual in nature because it ministers to the soul and comforts the human spirit, but without religion or preaching. Spirituality is about existential meaning, purpose, living life to its fullest, and taking care of ourselves and those around us whom we care about. In this conceptual context, spirituality is a wholesome, vital ingredient to stress management and wellness. Spirituality is distinctly different from religion, which tends to focus on doctrine.

The hope we offer to others is priceless! Sometimes we feel helpless and inadequate to offer help, unqualified to promote healing that encompasses body, soul, and spirit. The smallest things, however, can be meaningful and nurturing. Sometimes just standing beside someone and sharing their pain is therapeutic. It represents what the Great Physician might do. The following anecdotal event offers an excellent behavioral example of sagacious spirituality.

A family who recently moved into the neighborhood suddenly lost a son to an unexpected death. The family was stricken with immense grief and sorrow. The lady across the street wanted to stand with her new neighbor and support her in some way. On a whim she asked the grieving mother if she would like to go for a walk. Her neighbor agreed. The two ladies walked for several miles and neither one said a word during their entire three-hour walk. The walk was therapeutic but it was more than just a walk; it was part of a healing journey that led to recovery. Over time, the two eventually became friends. This represents the essence of a priceless gift, by standing with and beside someone who is grieving, yet not trying to fix them or intellectualize their pain. There is a pain that words cannot describe. There is a pain that words alone cannot heal.

This book by Dr. Kate Hendricks Thomas will change the way you look at warriors, and perhaps even the way you look at life and adversity. Dr. Thomas has the educational training, skill, field experience, and expository teaching insight to analytically assess the stigma and subculture issues that warriors battle, and the specious cognitive thinking warriors embrace, which repeatedly manifests a disinclination to seek professional treatment that would help them. This book will open your eyes to ways in which we can reach out to warriors and support them with pragmatic, tactical intervention, healing, and love that is transformational.

Mark Malmin
Author, consultant, public speaker on warrior culture, stress management, spirituality
www.MarkMalmin.com

ENDNOTES

Chapter 1

1. I borrow here from theorist Sandra Harding's writings on embodied knowledge. It is "a way of experiencing a relationship to history, to divinity, to ancestry from within movements of one's own body, from within the deepest memories of one's own cells."
    *   S. Harding, "Standpoint theories: Productively controversial," *Hypatia*, 24:4 (2009): 192–200.

2. Dr. Lissa Rankin is a registered MD who has become keenly interested in holistic wellness, particularly in the ways that our spiritual health impacts us physically. She started the Whole Health Medicine Institute to train fellow physicians and has authored books on the subject.
    *   L. Rankin, *The Fear Cure: Cultivating Courage as Medicine for the Body, Mind, and Soul* (Carlsbad, CA: Hay House, 2015).

3. Eric Greitens is a Navy Seal and the founder of The Mission Continues, a nonprofit that funds fellowships for military veterans engaged in community service work. His work explicitly embraces a narrative of purpose and challenge for military personnel transitioning to civilian life and provides a stirring take on the issue.
    *   E. Greitens, *Resilience: Hard-Won Wisdom for Living a Better Life* (Boston, MA: Houghton Mifflin Harcourt, 2015).
    *   E. Greitens, *The Heart and the Fist: The Education of a Humanitarian, the Making of a Navy SEAL* (Boston, MA: Houghton Mifflin Harcourt, 2011).

4. Posttraumatic growth is a phrase with specific meaning. People can grow in radical, positive ways from struggling through hard times. Scholars systematically studying this process and these mechanisms for growth are working on theoretical models that may someday be useful to design programs for trauma sufferers that emphasize strength through adversity.
   - R. G. Tedeschi and L. G. Calhoun, "Posttraumatic growth: Conceptual foundations and empirical evidence," *Psychological Inquiry*, 15:1 (2004): 1–18.

Chapter 2

1. Statistics on the active duty military and veteran populations are tracked and reported by numerous agencies:
   - Defense Manpower Data Center. (2012). *2011 Demographics Report*. Office of the Deputy Under-Secretary of Defense (Military Community and Family Policy).
   - Department of Defense. "The challenge and the promise: Strengthening the force, preventing suicide, and saving lives—final report of the DOD task force on the prevention of suicide by members of the armed forces." Accessed December 7, 2013, Available at: http://www.health.mil/dhb/downloads
   - United States Census Bureau. (2014). "Statistical abstract of the United States." Available at: http://www.census.gov/compendia/statab/2012/tables/12s0521.pdf

Chapter 3

1. There have been outstanding analyses of the problems with mental health diagnoses in military personnel by former service physicians. Stress injury looks like depression, and the symptoms work well in an intense environment. In many ways, these mental health "problems" are absolutely adaptive.
   - C. W. Hoge, *Once a Warrior, Always a Warrior,* 1st ed. (Guilford, CT: Lyons Press, 2010).
   - C. W. Hoge and C. A. Castro, "Preventing suicides in US

service members and veterans." *Journal of American Medical Association*, 308:7 (2012): 671–672.

2. Understanding the ways in which depression and stress injuries are categorized in the clinical setting is complicated, as symptoms vary between patients and the conditions often either co-occur or look markedly similar.
   - R. M. Bossarte, Ed., *Veterans Suicide: A Public Health Imperative*, 1st ed. (Washington D.C.: American Public Health Association, 2013).
   - P. S. Calhoun, J. S. Hertzberg, A. C. Kirby, M. F. Dennis, L. P. Hair, E. A. Dedert, and J. C. Beckham, "The effect of draft DSM-V criteria on posttraumatic stress disorder prevalence." *Depression & Anxiety*, 29:12 (2012): 1032–1042.
   - *Diagnostic and Statistical Manual of Mental Disorders: DSM-5.* Washington, D.C.: American Psychiatric Association, c2013.

3. The human stress response is a normal adaptation meant to keep us safe in reaction to a perceived threat. It only becomes a health problem when it doesn't shut off. This can occur when a stressor is so traumatic that the brain keeps reexperiencing it, or when stressors are chronic.
   - J. A. Romas, and M. Sharma, *Practical Stress Management: A Comprehensive Workbook for Promoting Health and Managing Change through Stress Reduction* (5th ed.) (San Francisco, CA: Benjamin Cummings, 2010).
   - B. Seaward, *Managing Stress: Principles and Strategies for Health and Well-being* (Sudbury, Mass.: Jones and Bartlett, 2004).

4. Studies on the impact of stress show that unchecked fight or flight-level responses impair us on both physiological and neurological levels. Interestingly, this can be reversed by using relaxation techniques to activate the parasympathetic nervous system and calm the stress response. That is why we often hear that taking time to relax can make us mentally sharper; it actually changes our brain tissue!
   - A. P. Jha and A. Kiyonaga, "Working-memory-triggered dynamic adjustments in cognitive control." *Journal of*

Experimental Psychology: Learning, Memory, and Cognition, 36:4 (2010): 1036–1042.

- A. P. Jha, E. A. Stanley, A. Kiyonaga, L. Wong, and L. Gelfand, L. "Examining the protective effects of mindfulness training on working memory capacity and affective experience." *Emotion*, 10:1(2010): 54–64.
- J.J. Vasterling, S. P. Proctor, P. Amoroso, R. Kane, T. Heeren, and R. F. White. "Neuropsychological outcomes of army personnel following deployment to the Iraq war." *Journal of the American Medical Association* 296: 5 (2006): 519-529.

5. We don't really know how many veterans are suffering from stress injuries because they are notoriously misunderstood, misdiagnosed, and stigmatized. Ranges vary from 15–50 percent depending on the source.
    - J. Acosta, K. Reynolds, E. M. Gillen, K. C. Feeney, C. M. Farmer, and R. M. Weinick, *The RAND Online Measure Repository for Evaluating Psychological Health and Traumatic Brain Injury Programs* (Washington, D.C.: RAND Corporation, 2014).
    - S. S. Coughlin, Ed. *Posttraumatic Stress Disorder and Chronic Health Conditions*, 1st ed. (Washington D.C.: American Public Health Association, 2012).
    - Department of Veterans Affairs. "Mental Health and Military Sexual Trauma." Accessed January 12, 2014, Available at http://www.mentalhealth.va.gov/msthome.asp

6. Cooperating socially and experiencing social support in a warm community are adaptive behaviors for which we are wired. Studies have shown that close networks in faith communities increase life expectancy by as much as 7.5 years, and people without strong social networks fare worse when recovering from injury or surgery. To lose community is the ultimate stressor for a brain wired for connection, and that is exactly what veterans experience when they leave the military and return to a civilian world that may no longer feel like home. Transition, then, becomes a traumatic stressor.
    - Sebastian Junger, "How PTSD became a problem far beyond the battlefield." *Vanity Fair* (June 2015). Retrieved from: http://www.vanityfair.com/news/2015/05/ptsd-war-home-sebastian-junger

- Rob Moll, *What Your Body Knows about God: How We Are Designed to Connect, Serve, and Thrive* (Downers Grove: IL: InterVarsity Press, 2014).

7. Research into stress injury and depression prevalence has identified some of the issues the services face with these mental health conditions as they relate to combat deployments. Interestingly, deploying doesn't make problems more likely than remaining in garrison.
   - M. A. Ilgen, J. F. McCarthy, R. V. Ignacio, A. B. Bohnert, M. Valenstein, F. C. Blow, and I. R. Katz, "Psychopathology, Iraq and Afghanistan service, and suicide among Veterans Health Administration patients." *Journal of Consulting and Clinical Psychology* 80:3 (2012): 323–330.
   - K. H. Seal, T. J. Metzler, K. S. Gima, D. Bertenthal, S. Maguen, and C. R. Marmar, (2009). "Trends and risk factors for mental health diagnoses among Iraq and Afghanistan veterans using Department of Veterans Affairs health care." *American Journal of Public Health* 99:9, (2002–2008): 1651–1658.
   - T. Tanielan, and L. H. Jaycox, *Invisible Wounds of War: Psychological and Cognitive Injuries, Their Consequences, and Services to Assist Recovery* (Washington, D.C.: RAND Corporation, 2008).

8. Qualitative studies that ask in-depth questions often find that veterans feel deeply alienated from non-veterans.
   - L. A. Brenner, and S. M. Barnes, (2012). "Facilitating treatment engagement during high- risk transition periods: A potential suicide prevention strategy." *American Journal of Public Health* 102 (2012): S12–S14.
   - P. M. Gutierrez, L. A. Brenner, J. A. Rings, M. D. Devore, P. J. Kelly, P. J. Staves, and M. S. Kaplan, "A qualitative description of female veterans' deployment-related experiences and potential suicide risk factors." *Journal of Clinical Psychology*, 69:9 (2013): 923–935.

9. The University of Alabama is working to build collaborative partnerships to study military veteran transitions with interdisciplinary faculty from social work, psychology, education, and health sciences. Researchers there are working to expand translational research

on veteran transitions in the southeastern United States. In 2015 and 2016, they hosted summits funded by a National Institute of Mental Health grant to bring veterans, researchers, clinicians, and practitioners together to offer new perspectives on streamlining veteran transitions.

- The Service Member to Civilian (S2C) Summit hosted by UA has a website: https://www.facebook.com/UAS2CSummit
- K. Hendricks Thomas, L. W. Turner, A. Paschal, A. Knowlden, and D. A. Birch, "Predictors of depression diagnoses and symptoms in veterans: Results from a national survey," *Military Behavioral Health*, doi/full/10.1080/2163578 1.2015.1085928.
- K. Hendricks Thomas, L. W. Turner, and Taylor S. Plummer (April 2015). *Predictors of depression diagnoses in veterans: Results from a national survey.* Annual Conference for the Society of Public Health Education, Portland, OR (oral presentation).

Chapter 4

1. The stigma faced by service members seeking health care for depression and posttraumatic stress has been well documented. In addition to the cultural norms that disparage the conditions as failures or weaknesses, structural repercussions discourage care-seeking. Peers and commanders at times ridicule or punish members who have chosen to identify themselves in need of help in both formal and informal ways. Many serving legitimately fear patient identity, as it may harm career advancement.

- Y. Dreazen, *The Invisible Front* (New York, NY: Crown Publishers, 2014).
- C. W. Hoge, and C. A. Castro, (2012). "Preventing suicides in US service members and veterans," *Journal of American Medical Association* 308:7 (2012): 671–672.
- VA Mental Health (VAMH). (2011). *Number of veterans receiving care, barriers faced, and efforts to increase access.* U.S. Government Accountability Office. Accessed June 17, 2015. Available at: http://www.gao.gov/assets/590/585743.pdf

2. The push and pull of our environment shape our notions of self and how that self should interact with the world. Scholars and theorists have outlined in great detail the way that such environmental factors and social norms shape behavior.

   - S. Ahmed, *The Promise of Happiness* (Durham, NC: Duke University Press, 2010).
   - E. B. Shiraev and D. A. Levy, *Cross-cultural psychology: Critical thinking and contemporary applications* 4th edition ed. (Boston, MA: Pearson/Allyn Bacon, 2010).

3. Through case study, observation, and program analysis, Mark Malmin's work to explain the rigid norms of law enforcement and military culture translates member behavior for the civilian reader and offers a foundational understanding of the culture's insularity and tendencies toward treatment-avoidance.

   - M. M. Malmin, "Warrior culture, spirituality, and prayer," *Journal of Religion and Health* 52:3 (2013): 740–758.

4. Studies both quantitative and qualitative in nature have thoroughly documented the issue of mental health care avoidance and problems with treatment program adherence in the military and veteran populations. Military personnel cite a variety of reasons for not seeking available care, from fear of reprisal to denial of symptom presence.

   - S. S. Coughlin, Ed. *Posttraumatic Stress Disorder and Chronic Health Conditions* (1st ed.) (Washington D.C.: American Public Health Association, 2012).
   - J. M. Currier, J. M. Holland, and D. Allen, "Attachment and mental health symptoms among U.S. Afghanistan and Iraq veterans seeking health care services," *Journal of Traumatic Stress*, 25:6 (2012): 633–640.
   - C. A. Elnitsky, E. M. Andresen, M. E. Clark, S. McGarity, C. G. Hall, and R. D. Kerns, "Access to the US department of Veterans Affairs health system: Self-reported barriers to care among returnees of Operations Enduring Freedom and Iraqi Freedom," *BMC Health Services Research*, 13:1 (2013): 1–20.
   - K. H. Koo, "Military sexual trauma and mental health diagnoses in female veterans returning from Afghanistan

and Iraq: Barriers and facilitators to Veterans Affairs care," *Hastings Women's Law Journal* 25 (2014): 25–27.

5. An insular culture breeds an "us vs. them" mentality and creates palpable disconnect from civilian society that makes reintegration after deployment or even garrison service difficult. This disconnect can create feelings of alienation, exacerbate symptoms of depression or posttraumatic stress, and generate even more barriers to seeking treatment.
   • L. A. Brenner, and S. M. Barnes, "Facilitating treatment engagement during high- risk transition periods: A potential suicide prevention strategy," *American Journal of Public Health* 102 (2012): S12–S14.
   • C. W. Hoge, *Once a Warrior, Always a Warrior* 1st ed. (Guilford, CT: Lyons Press, 2010).
   • Department of Defense. *The challenge and the promise: Strengthening the force, preventing suicide, and saving lives - final report of the DOD task force on the prevention of suicide by members of the armed forces.* Accessed December 7, 2013, Available at: http://www.health.mil/dhb/downloads

6. A combat stress mental health provider for the Marines of Al Anbar in 2004, Dr. Heidi Squier Kraft wrote a powerful memoir of her experiences. Her work is the best I have read to date in terms of helping others understand the cultural disconnect faced by service members returning to a civilian community far removed from the wars in Iraq and Afghanistan.
   • H. Squier Kraft, *Rule Number Two: Lessons Learned in a Combat Hospital* (New York, NY: Back Bay Books, 2007).

7. The notion that deployment and combat trauma are the primary causes of stress injury and depression in veterans has been largely discredited by recent research. A far more important predictor of such conditions is a recent separation from service, in particular a separation that involved any sort of discipline problems. Those discipline problems may be the result of maladaptive behaviors related to stress injury, as behaviors suitable in a combat environment are not at all suitable for garrison.

- J. Friedman, "Risk factors for suicide among army personnel," *Journal of the American Medical Association* 11 (2015): 1154–1155.
- Sebastian Junger, (June 2015). How PTSD became a problem far beyond the battlefield. *Vanity Fair.* Retrieved from: http://www.vanityfair.com/news/2015/05/ptsd-war-home-sebastian-junger

Chapter 5

1. Resilience has been studied in many different populations, but common personality traits are typically identified in members of each community who demonstrate the quality. Because the traits can be identified, they can be trained and cultivated. Resilience can be taught.
   - I. Heavy Runner and K. Marshall, "Miracle survivors: Promoting resilience in Indian students," *Tribal College Journal* 14:4 (2003): 14–18.

2. Today, Sarah Plummer Taylor is an author, a health coach, speaker, and social worker who tirelessly serves her community of fellow veterans. She has done a great deal of advocacy work in the area of Military Sexual Trauma (MST), supporting Senator Gillibrand's efforts to get such felonies adjudicated outside the military chain of command.
   - www.sempersarah.com
   - S. Plummer Taylor, *Just Roll With It: The 7 Battle-Tested Traits for Creating a Ridiculously Happy, Healthy, and Successful Life* (Collierville, TN: Innovo Publishing, 2015).

3. Behavioral change theories help guide our understanding of how to conduct outreach in any population, and choosing one to underpin a program should be done with culture in mind.
   - J. Hayden, *Introduction to Health Behavior Theory* (Boston, MA US: Jones and Bartlett Publishers, 2009).
   - M. M. Malmin, "Warrior culture, spirituality, and prayer," *Journal of Religion and Health* 52:3 (2013): 740–758.

4. Posttraumatic growth is an oft-discussed concept that retains a focus on post-incident care and adaptation. It is wildly useful when thinking about veterans working to recover from something traumatic, but it

lends itself less to the general, preventive focus for which I wish to advocate in this book.

- B. Garcia and A. Petrovich, *Strengthening the DSM: Incorporating Resilience and Cultural Competence* (New York, NY: Springer, 2011).
- G. Richardson, "The metatheory of resilience and resiliency, *Journal of Clinical Psychology* 58:3 (2002): 307–321.

5. Resiliency has been extensively studied, and key traits make a person more resilient. Most of these traits are related to one's ability to demonstrate self-awareness, adapt, and communicate across difference.

- B. Bernard, *Turning It All Around for Youth: From Risk to Resilience* (Launceston, Tasmania: Resiliency Associates and Global Learning Communities, 1997).
- J. Fleming and R. J. Ledogar "Resilience, an evolving concept: A review of literature relevant to aboriginal research," *Pimatisiwin: Journal of aboriginal and indigenous community health* 6:2 (2008): 7–23.
- N. Garmenzy, "Resiliency and vulnerability to adverse developmental outcomes associated with poverty," *American Behavioral Scientist* 34 (1991): 416–430.
- M. Rutter, "Resilience in the face of adversity: Protective factors and resistance to psychiatric disorder," *British Journal of Psychiatry* 147 (1985): 598–611.
- E. Werner and R. Smith, *Vulnerable but Invincible: A Longitudinal Study of Children and Youth* (Ithaca, NY: McGraw Hill, 1982).

6. We adapt to stress and can train for hardship.

- L. Rankin, *Mind Over Medicine: Scientific Proof You Can Heal Yourself* (Los Angeles, CA: Hay House, Inc., 2013).

7. Noted psychologists and psychiatrists have suggested that competency and resiliency characteristics are strengths that are more protective than risk-reduction efforts when it comes to depression. Tested specifically for validity in military communities, protective effects against depression most often emphasize adaptability.

- D. Fletcher and M. Sarkar, "Psychological resilience: A review and critique of definitions, concepts, and theory," *European Psychologist* 18:1 (2013): 12–23.

- G. Richardson, B. Neiger, S. Jensen, and K. Kumpfer, "The resiliency model," *Health Education* 21:6 (1990): 33–39.
- H. M. Foran, A. B. Adler, D. McGurk, and P. D. Bliese, "Soldiers' perceptions of resilience training and postdeployment adjustment: Validation of a measure of resilience training content and training process," *Psychological Services* 9:4 (2012): 390–403.
- K. Hendricks Thomas and S. Plummer Taylor, "Beyond Trauma Treatment: Mindfulness Instruction in the Training Environment to Prevent Depression, Lower Suicide Rates and Improve Resilience in the Military and Veteran Communities," *Journal of Traumatic Stress Disorders and Treatment* 4:2 (2015): 1–4.
- L. Whiting, S. Kendall, and W. Wills, "An asset-based approach: An alternative health promotion strategy," *Community Practitioner* 85:1 (2012): 25–37.

8. Studies have shown that military personnel in possession of known resilient traits rarely suffer problems after deployment.
   - J. H. Lee, S. K. Nam, A. Kim, B. Kim, M. Y. Lee, and S. M. Lee, "Resilience: A meta-analytic approach," *Journal of Counseling & Development* 91:3 (2013): 269–279.
   - R. H. Pietrzak, D. C. Johnson, M. B. Goldstein, J. C. Malley, and S. M. Southwick, "Psychological resilience and postdeployment social support protect against traumatic stress and depressive symptoms in soldiers returning from Operations Enduring Freedom and Iraqi Freedom," *Depression and Anxiety* 26:8 (2009): 745–751.

9. Empirically validating programs designed to build resilience is an exciting and emerging effort for behavioral health professionals.
   - K. Hendricks Thomas, S. Plummer Taylor, K. Hamner, J. Glazer, and E. Kaufman, "Multi-site programming offered to promote resilience in military veterans: A process evaluation of the Just Roll With it Bootcamps," *Californian Journal of Health Promotion* 13:2 (2015) 15–24.

- K. Lehavot, T. L. Simpson, C. Der-Martirosian, J. C. Shipherd, and D. L. Washington, (2013). "The role of military social support in understanding the relationship between PTSD, physical health, and healthcare utilization in women veterans," *Journal of Traumatic Stress* 34 (2013): 111–117.
- D. Libby, E. Corey, and R. Desai, "Complementary and alternative medicine in VA specialized PTSD treatment programs," *Psychiatric Services* 63:11 (2012): 1134–1136.
- T. Nassif, D. Norris, M. Gomez, R. Karch, and J. Chapman, *Examining the Effectiveness of Mindfulness Meditation in Combat Veterans with Traumatic Brain Injury* (American University, Washington D.C., 2013).

Chapter 6

1. A 2015 article in the *Los Angeles Times* highlighted the cultural and geographic schism that currently exists between mainstream civilian society and the military. Less than one-half of 1 percent of the US population is in the armed services today, and most service members hail from southern states and families with military service histories. There is truly a divide.
   - D. Zucchino, (May 25, 2015). US military and civilians are increasingly divided. *Los Angeles Times*. Retrieved from: http://m.military.com/daily-news/2015/05/25/us-military-and-civilians-are-increasingly-divided.html?ESRC=todayinmil.sm.

2. A warm thank-you must be extended to Blayne Smith of TeamRWB and Christine Fennessy of *Runner's World*. Blayne's original interview was written by Christine in narrative form and posted on the TeamRWB blog; her moving and skillful writing and his personal story have been adapted and expanded and is shared with their permission.
   - C. Fennessy and B. Smith, (February 27, 2014). Blayne Smith—A soldier, in parts. *The Team Red, White, & Blue Blog*. Retrieved from: www.teamrwb.org/blog.

3. Stress injury leads to emotional reactivity and a decline in the ability to connect with others, feel compassion, and interact in socially

normative ways. This often creates a vicious cycle for veterans coping with trauma; the social support they desperately need to recover is lost in the close relationships damaged by existing symptoms.

- S. Cohen, L. Underwood, and B. H. Gottlieb, *Social Support Measurement and Intervention: A Guide for Health and Social Scientists* (New York, NY: Oxford University Press, 2000).
- J. M. Currier, J. M. Holland, and D. Allen, "Attachment and mental health symptoms among U.S. Afghanistan and Iraq veterans seeking health care services," *Journal of Traumatic Stress* 25:6 (2012): 633–640.
- C. E. Cutrona, *Social support in couples: marriage as a resource in times of stress* (Thousand Oaks, CA: Sage Publications, 1996).

4. Social cohesion reduces stress levels in humans; we are wired for connection and cooperation. The research basis for such a claim is extensive; well-connected people live longer and suffer less illness and disease than people who are lonely. Specifically looking at mental health conditions like depression and anxiety, the results are dramatic. Support yields trackable physiological, mental, and emotional benefits!

- B. Egolf, J. Lasker, S. Wolf, and L. Potvin, "The Roseto Effect: A 50-Year Comparison of Mortality Rates," *American Journal of Public Health* 82:8 (1992): 1089–1098.
- J. S. Goodwin, W. C. Hunt, C. R. Key, and J. M. Samet, "The effect of marital status on stage, treatment, and survival of cancer patients," *Journal of the American Medical Association* 258:21 (1987): 3125–3130.
- B. R. Sarason, I. G. Sarason, and G. R. Pierce, *Social support: An interactional view* (Hoboken, NJ: John Wiley & Sons, 1990).

5. Even if relationships are not friction-free, constant interaction with family and friends yields protective health benefits and builds our capacity to grow through trauma. "Protective effects" is an epidemiological phrase meaning that a given behavior or demographic variable makes a health issue less likely to occur. Of course, this is not a guarantee. Partnered and connected people will get ill, but much like a nonsmoker is less likely to develop emphysema; connected individuals are less likely to suffer from a host of health issues.

- A. J. Smith, C. C. Benight, and R. Cieslak, "Social support and postdeployment coping self-efficacy as predictors of distress among combat veterans," *Military Psychology,* 25:5 (2013): 452–461.

6. Team Red, White, and Blue (TeamRWB) is a true community-based veterans' service organization (VSO) and my favorite group with which to spend my time and energy. Their mission is to enrich the lives of America's veterans by connecting them to their community through physical and social activity.
   - www.teamrwb.org

Chapter 7

1. Wellness texts that treat health like a topic with many components and discuss holistic principles are ones worth reading.
   - S. Plummer Taylor and K. Hendricks Thomas, *Just Roll With It Wellness Journal* (Tuscaloosa, AL: Resilience Press, 2014).
     - K. Hendricks Thomas and S. Plummer Taylor, "A feminist approach to wellness," *Gender Forum, Early Career Researchers Special Issue,* 45(1), Retrieved from http://www.genderforum.org/issues/special-issue-early-career-researchers-i/re-thinking-wellness-a-feminist-approach-to-health-and-fitness/

2. Health problems are an undeniable result of chronic stress, which decreases a person's resilience.
   - K. T. Larkin, *Stress and Hypertension: Examining the Relation between Psychological Stress and High Blood Pressure* (New Haven, CT: Yale University Press, 2005).
   - J. Romas and M. Sharma, *Practical Stress Management* 5th ed. (San Francisco, CA: Benjamin Cummings, 2010).
   - Brian Seaward, *Managing Stress* 7th ed. (Burlington, MA: Jones and Bartlett, 2010).

3. The benefits of clean eating and physical exercise are many, and such self-care practices have been linked to improved health. They offer protective effects from illness and disease as well as improved

quality of life indicators. Mental health improves with better care of the physical self, particularly with depression and anxiety. Both clean eating and mindful movement practices lower stress levels and create a physical platform capable of demonstrating resilience when need arises.

- M. H. Anshel, M. Kang, and T. M. Brinthaupt, "A values-based approach for changing exercise and dietary habits: An action study," *International Journal of Sport & Exercise Psychology* 8:4 (2010): 413–432.

4. The physical practice of yoga has been proven to offer both the benefit of a fitness modality with the stress relief of prayer or quiet contemplation. Stress-related illness is a modern epidemic. According to the American Medical Association, three out of every four doctors' visits involve illnesses related to chronic stress. To complement traditional treatments, the utilization of the practice of yoga offers promise. Some VA hospitals conduct yoga and meditation seminars for patients suffering from a host of maladies.

- S. Evans, J. C. I. Tsao, B. Sternlieb, and L. K. Zeltzer, "Using the biopsychosocial model to understand the health benefits of yoga," *Journal of Complementary & Integrative Medicine* 6:1 (2009): 1–22.
- D. Farhi, *Yoga Mind, Body, and Spirit* 1st ed. (New York, NY: Holt, 2000).
- J. Granath and S. Ingvarsson, "Stress management: A randomized study of cognitive behavioural therapy and yoga," *Cognitive Behavior Therapy* 35:1 (2007)
- K. Hendricks Thomas and S. Plummer Taylor, "Beyond Trauma Treatment: Mindfulness Instruction in the Training Environment to Prevent Depression, Lower Suicide Rates and Improve Resilience in the Military and Veteran Communities," *Journal of Traumatic Stress Disorders and Treatment* 4:2 (2015): 1–4.
- K. Hendricks Thomas, L. Turner, and S. Hunt, "Integrating yoga into stress-reduction interventions: Application of the health belief model," *Arkansas Journal of Health Promotion* 49 (2014): 55–60.

- S. Smeeding, D. H. Bradshaw, K. L. Kumpfer, S. Trevithick, and G. J. Stoddard, "Outcome evaluation of the Veterans Affairs Salt Lake City Integrative Health Clinic for chronic nonmalignant pain," *The Clinical Journal of Pain* 27 (2011): 146–155.

5. Healthy behaviors are linked to better mental health status. In the diet, this means limiting alcohol and eating clean foods. Physically, this means adopting balanced activity programs.
   - A. Harrington, *The Cure Within: A History of Mind-Body Medicine* (New York, NY: WW Norton & Company, 2008).
   - H. G. Koenig, Ed., *Handbook of Religion and Mental Health* (West Conshohocken, PA: Elsevier, 1998).

6. Dr. Theresa Larson is a veteran and DPT who runs a physical therapy business in San Diego that caters to athletes and Wounded Warriors. She volunteers extensively with adaptive functional fitness efforts that work to bring movement opportunities to people completing physical rehabilitation programs at the local military hospital.
   - http://www.drtheresalarson.com/

Chapter 8

1. Understanding the way we use the terms religious and spiritual are important when we discuss the importance of faith to health and resilience. In this chapter, I am explicitly talking about the utility of believing, belonging, and participating in an organized faith community.
   - H. G. Koenig, "Concerns about measuring 'spirituality' in research," *The Journal of Nervous and Mental Disease* 196:5 (2008): 349–355.

2. Faith improves a person's health both mentally and physically and has been shown to be tremendously beneficial for individuals coping with stressful or traumatic events. Neuroscientists are discovering that a belief in a higher power and moral code can be physiologically beneficial in a very trackable way.
   - S. Dein, C. C. Cook, A. Powell, and S. Eagger, "Religion, spirituality and mental health," *The Psychiatrist* 34:2 (2010): 63–64.

- H. G. Koenig, M. E. McCullough, and D. B. Larson, *Handbook of Religion and Health* (Oxford, England: Oxford University Press, 2001).
- W. L. Larimore, M. Parker, and M. Crowther, "Should clinicians incorporate positive spirituality into their practices? What does the evidence say?" *Annals of Behavioral Medicine* 24:1 (2002): 69–73.

3. Studies on religion and mental health demonstrate that it helps people cope, connect, and make healthier choices.
   - H. G. Keonig, *Medicine, Religion, and Health: Where Science and Spirituality Meet* (West Conshohocken, PA: Templeton Press, 2008).

4. Pastor Chris Hodges leads the Church of the Highlands in Birmingham, Alabama. Before moving to South Carolina, this was my family's former church home and the place where our son was dedicated. Pastor Chris' writing about the joy, energy, vitality, and purpose that belonging to a life-giving church brings is uniquely relevant to this conversation about faith's role in building resilience. His church focuses heavily on connection in small groups, communicating in welcoming fashion with anyone and everyone, and community service.
   - C. Hodges, *Fresh Air: Trading Stale Spiritual Obligation for a Life-Altering, Energizing, Experience-It-Everyday Relationship with God* (Carol Stream, IL: Tyndale Publishers, 2012).

5. Active duty military personnel are often more likely to speak with chaplains than mental health providers. As such, chaplains are an important referral source for service members who need help for stress injuries or mental health problems like depression.
   - M. S. Kopacz and M. J. Pollitt, "Delivering chaplaincy services to veterans at increased risk of suicide," *Journal of Health Care Chaplaincy* 21:1 (2015): 1–13.
   - J. A. Nieuwsma, J. E. Rhodes, G. L. Jackson, W. C. Cantrell, M. E. Lane, M. J. Bates, and K. G. Meador, "Chaplaincy and mental health in the Department of Veterans Affairs and Department of Defense," *Journal of Health Care Chaplaincy* 19:1 (2013): 3–21.

6. Sarah Bessey is a Christian author who writes about finding Christianity as Jesus taught it, often outside traditional dogmatic lines. She writes movingly about the way both motherhood and service efforts have impacted her faith journey.
   - S. Bessey, *Jesus Feminist: An Invitation to Revisit the Bible's View of Women* (New York, NY: Simon and Schuster, 2013).
   - www.sarahbessey.com

7. Biofeedback has provided neurologists with fascinating evidence that faith practices optimize our mental and physical health. We are wired for connection with God and with one another. Simple companionship doesn't yield the same effects that faith communities offer; such soul connections look entirely different on a functional MRI or PET scan.
   - P. Haas, *Pharisectomy: How to Joyfully Remove Your Inner Pharisee and Other Religiously Transmitted Diseases* (Springfield, MO: Influence Resources, 2012).
   - M. E. Koltko-Rivera, "Rediscovering the later version of Maslow's hierarchy of needs: Self-transcendence and opportunities for theory, research, and unification," *Review of General Psychology* 10:4 (2006): 302.
   - Rob Moll, *What Your Body Knows about God: How We Are Designed to Connect, Serve, and Thrive* (Downers Grove: IL: InterVarsity Press, 2014).
   - A. Newberg and E. G. d'Aquili, *Why God Won't Go Away: Brain Science and the Biology of Belief* (New York, NY: Ballantine Books, 2008).

8. Worthy reading for anyone interested in resilience are books by scholar Brene Brown, PhD. She asks important questions about how authentically we connect with others and with God and has coined the term *wholeheartedness* to describe people who display high levels of resilience and self-reported quality of life.
   - B. Brown, *The Gifts of Imperfection: Let Go of Who You Think You're Supposed to Be and Embrace Who You Are* (Center City, MN: Hazeldon Publishing, 2013).

9. Faith optimizes individual health and creates a ripple effect in larger communities. This shows up in volunteer work, charitable outreach,

and reductions in crime, alcohol abuse rates, and substance abuse. There are several outstanding books on the subject of altruism as it relates to religiosity well worth reviewing!

- R. D. Putnam, *Bowling Alone: The Collapse and Revival of American Community* (New York, NY: Simon and Schuster, 2001).
- A. L. Sherman, *Kingdom Calling: Vocational Stewardship for the Common Good* (Downers Grove, IL: InterVarsity Press, 2011).
- P. Yancey and P. Brand, *Fearfully and Wonderfully Made* (Nashville, TN: Zondervan, 2010).

10. Theosomatic medicine is a fascinating and evolving field that explores energy, consciousness, and divine influence on the human body.

- J. Levin, *God, Faith, and Health: Exploring the Spirituality-Healing Connection* (Hoboken, NJ: John Wiley & Sons, 2002).

11. Studies done on the utility of prayer on health and healing make for fascinating reading. Whether researchers attribute the results they have found to subtle energy flows or the blessing of an omnipotent God, they create space for considering spirituality's role in health, healing, and wellness.

- D. J. Benor, *Healing Research: Holistic Energy Medicine and Spirituality* (West Bloomfield, MI: Helix Publishing, 1993).

12. Studies are not completely conclusive, and researchers are cautious about making sweeping statements about divine intervention in healing. The question must be asked about whether the scientific method can even be applied to conceptualizing divinity. In truth, the debates rage in both the theological and clinical communities and at times become quite hotly contested.

- K. S. Masters and G. I. Spielmans, "Prayer and health: review, meta-analysis, and research agenda," *Journal of Behavioral Medicine* 30:4 (2007): 329–338.
- K. S. Masters, "Research on the healing power of distant intercessory prayer: Disconnect between science and faith," *Journal of Psychology and Theology* 33:4 (2005): 268.
- M. E. McCullough, "Prayer and health: Conceptual issues, research review, and research agenda," *Journal of Psychology and Theology* 23:1 (1995): 15–29.

Chapter 9

1. My research on depression rates in military veterans has shown that the most likely group of veterans to self-report symptoms that indicate undiagnosed depression of mild, moderate, or major severity is the most recent cohort of service members from the Iraq and Afghanistan conflict era. These veterans are more likely to be newly transitioning and less likely to have successfully navigated access to care issues with the DOD or VA. They also combat strong stigma against mental health care seeking. In a sample of over 54,000 veterans, only 2.2 percent agreed or strongly agreed that mental health treatment was useful, and 97.8 percent held unfavorable opinions on getting clinical help for mental health struggles.

    - K. Hendricks Thomas, L. W. Turner, A. Paschal, A. Knowlden, and D. A. Birch, "Predictors of depression diagnoses and symptoms in veterans: Results from a national survey," *Military Behavioral Health*, doi/full/10.1080/2163578 1.2015.1085928

    - K. Hendricks Thomas, L. W. Turner, and S. Plummer Taylor, (April 2015). *Predictors of Depression Diagnoses in Veterans: Results from a National Survey.* Annual Conference for the Society of Public Health Education, Portland, OR (oral presentation).

2. Common transition training for the active component includes a one-week class that all service members complete as they end their time in service. Military personnel receive a great deal of information in firehouse fashion during these transition assistance classes. Opinions on program utility in veteran service spaces are typically that they do not offer a true bridge between the worlds.

3. Our resilience-building programs are called *Just Roll With It Bootcamps* and have been offered in seminar and retreat format domestically and internationally in partnership with some terrific veteran service organizations. We are always working to expand the care continuum and improve evaluation rigor. Our latest published results and the theoretical basis for our curriculum are available online.

    - www.justrollwithitwellness.com

- K. Hendricks Thomas, S. Plummer Taylor, K. Hamner, J. Glazer, and E. Kaufman, "Multi-site programming offered to promote resilience in military veterans: A process evaluation of the Just Roll With it Bootcamps" *Californian Journal of Health Promotion,* 13:2 (2015): 15–24.
- K. Hendricks Thomas, E. Kaufman, S. Plummer Taylor, K. Hamner, and J. Glazer, (June 2015). *Combatting suicide rates through programming offered to promote resilience in military veterans: An issue overview and process evaluation of the Just Roll With it Bootcamps.* Annual College of Charleston Conference on Suicide Prevention, Charleston, SC (oral presentation).

4. Because of military culture insularity, programs that seek to collaborate, bridge gaps, and use peer leadership meet with real success. As has been demonstrated successfully in recovery communities, peer mentoring and leadership provides the interaction, camaraderie, and instructor credibility required to sell an intervention to potentially recalcitrant participants in very specific, insular, or marginalized communities.

- J. F. Greden, M. Valenstein, J. Spinner, A. Blow, L. A. Gorman, G. W. Dalack, and M. Kees, "Buddy-to-buddy, a citizen soldier peer support program to counteract stigma, PTSD, depression, and suicide," *Annals of the New York Academy of Sciences* 1208 (2010): 90–97.
- P. M. Gutierrez, L. A. Brenner, J. A. Rings, M. D. Devore, P. J. Kelly, P. J. Staves, and M. S. Kaplan, "A qualitative description of female veterans' deployment-related experiences and potential suicide risk factors," *Journal of Clinical Psychology* 69:9 (2013): 923–935.
- P. Held and G. P. Owens, "Stigmas and attitudes toward seeking mental health treatment in a sample of veterans and active duty service members," *Traumatology* 19:2 (2013): 136–145.

5. Common military acronyms become like words in their own right to military members, especially in a deployed environment. Soldiers like Roger would potentially need a translator with civilian friends.

- Area of Operations (AO)
- Explosive Ordinance Disposal (EOD)
- Main Supply Route (MSR)

6. Dr. Kaplan's work out of Manhattan College is impressive, creative, and demonstrates a real concern for not just retention of student veterans but for quality of life improvement in the population.
    - I. Angell, (June 25, 2015). For Jasper vets, yoga is no stretch. *The Riverdale Press.* Retrieved from http://www.riverdalepress. com/stories/For-Jasper-vets-yoga-is-no-stretch,57287.
    - https://manhattan.edu/faculty/stephenkaplan

7. The Mind Fitness Training Institute team conducted a specific study on a company of Marines in the fleet during predeployment workups, seeking to answer the question of whether a mindfulness-based behavioral health intervention could improve the resilience of Marine Corps reservists preparing for a tour in Iraq and prevent depression problems after returning home. Attempting a mixed-methods approach to the explanatory/instrumental case study, the researchers studied one unit of thirty-four reservists in the predeployment workup phase. In addition to the normal training required before heading overseas, these reservists underwent a carefully tailored yoga and mindfulness program designed to improve their ability to manage both chronic and acute traumatic stress. Results were statistically significant in the studied population, demonstrating that adherence to intervention protocol for fifteen minutes each day exponentially improved working memory capacity. Working memory capacity contributes to emotional regulation as well as upper-level cognitive functioning. Such findings indicate an affirmative answer to the specific question of whether mindfulness training can promote stress resilience in a very specific population, at a very critical juncture.
    - Mind Fitness Training Institute: www.mind-fitness-training.org
    - A. P. Jha, E. A. Stanley, A. Kiyonaga, L. Wong, and L. Gelfand, L. "Examining the protective effects of mindfulness training on working memory capacity and affective experience," *Emotion* 10:1 (2010): 54–64.

- E. Teng, E. Hiatt, V. Mcclair, M. Kunik, M. Stanley, and B. Frueh, "Efficacy of posttraumatic stress disorder treatment for comorbid panic disorder: A critical review and future directions for treatment research," *Clinical Psychology: Science and Practice* 20:3 (2013): 268–284.

8. David Wood's journalism on moral injury is a tremendous resource important for understanding the way that military experiences can leave indelible impressions that negatively impact mental health and well-being in the future. His three-part series for *Huffington Post* can be read here: http://projects.huffingtonpost.com/moral-injury/the-grunts.

9. Designing programs without evaluation plans limits our ability to see if they work well, and our ability to use them on a larger scale should they meet with success. Too many resilience programs for military-connected personnel have not been evaluated carefully. Few programs (currently being delivered in piecemeal fashion) have any formal evaluation plan in place, though almost all those interviewed in the RAND study saw the need for longitudinal studies of the effectiveness of their programs.
   - S. S. Coughlin, Ed., *Post-Traumatic Stress Disorder and Chronic Health Conditions* 1st ed. (Washington D.C.: American Public Health Association, 2012).

Chapter 10

1. From Finding Valhalla's essay, *The Death of the Quiet Professional.* Available at http://findingvalhalla.com/2015/06/17/the-death-of-the-quiet-professional/ and completely worth reading.

2. Stress doesn't have to tear people down. Hardship and trauma can be the fires that hone focus and performance. It is all about mind-set.
   - K. McGonigal, *The Upside of Stress: Why Stress Is Good for You, and How to Get Good at It* (New York, NY: Avery Books, 2015).